RAIL CENTRES:
CREWE

RAIL CENTRES:
CREWE

REX CHRISTIANSEN

IAN ALLAN Publishing

Contents

First published 1993

ISBN 0 7110 2148 1

Published by Ian Allan Ltd, Shepperton, Surrey; and printed by Ian Allan Printing Ltd at their works at Coombelands in Runnymede, England.

1 Introduction 5

2 Birth and Growth of a
Great Railway Town 6

3 Junctions, North and South 10

4 Station 33

5 Independent Lines and Basford Hall
Marshalling Yard 40

6 25kV Electrification and Signalling 43

7 Passenger Services 53

8 Goods Services 76

9 Locomotive Works 81

10 Steam Sheds and Traction Depots 93

11 Locomotives 104

12 'The Railway Age' and
Forgotten Railways 117

13 Crewe Today 118

Appendices 123

Acknowledgements

Crewe deserves this book! Not because I have written it but because Crewe is so vibrant and enjoyable a railway town and junction. Many people have made delving into its history so much of a pleasure. Three friends have been of enormous help: Gordon Biddle and R. W. (Bob) Miller, both fellow authors, and Harold Forster MBE, retired Area Manager, Manchester Piccadilly, and formerly deputy AM, Crewe. They provided documents and photographs and drew on their own expert knowledge about many aspects of railways. I have also used material from the collection of the late Geoffrey Holt. I much appreciate the assistance of Tony Icke, Nigel Payton and Jim Peden. Some of the material I have used dates from modernisation three decades ago and I would like to thank BR staff with whom I worked while making electrification programmes for the BBC. Thanks to public affairs staff of InterCity, Regional Railways, Railfreight Distribution and Trainload Freight and ABB Transportation Ltd for help in bringing the Crewe story up to date.

Rex Christiansen
Chelford, Cheshire
January 1993

1 Introduction

Crewe station may lack the grandeur of York, its comparable 'half-way house' for Anglo-Scottish expresses on the East Coast main line, but it has a fascination that has delighted generations of enthusiasts. As a railway town it has an atmosphere that spreads far beyond its station and junctions and main lines.

It has seen the rise and decline of its railway works — now privatised — which once produced far more than locomotives. It has seen administrative changes. But its character, atmosphere and importance remain. To be in Crewe is to be in a town where it is hard not to be reminded of railways and their history.

All its junctions remain intact, and the quiet, flat countryside around the town remains largely unaltered, although a road has been opened up linking the M6 motorway with industrial Crewe and historic Nantwich — towns, which, since 1974, have formed one borough. The Chester and Shrewsbury lines run through the countryside of Cheshire and Shropshire to the Welsh border. On leaving Crewe, southbound InterCity passengers see miles of Staffordshire before they catch sight of a station — the usually deserted island platform of Norton Bridge.

To the north and east of Crewe and on the Kidsgrove line — the only route serving Crewe which is not classified as 'Principal' on BR passenger maps — there are small market and industrial towns that are still rail served.

People travel from them to work and shop in Crewe, but it remains a place which passengers see rather than visit, not least because the station and its modern town centre are a few minutes' bus ride apart. In some respects the most recent of the town's railway upheavals — the multi-million pound station and junction modernisation of 1985 — was designed to get people through Crewe more rapidly by upgrading the fast lines. It also allowed trains booked to stop there to get in and out of the station more quickly.

In *The Euston and Crewe Companion*, which he wrote in 1947, D. S. Barrie said the LMS main line between the two stations is surely as much entitled as any railway in the world to be called a great undertaking. Nearly fifty years on, as the line awaits further modernisation to cut the journey time between Glasgow and Euston to four hours and that between Euston and Manchester to 100min, few would disagree that the description is equally applicable to the line, and the station at Crewe, today.

2 Birth and Growth of a Great Railway Town

'Any one who studies a railway map of the United Kingdom will perceive that the London & North Western System, which extends nearly all over the country, from London in the south to Carlisle in the north, to Holyhead in the west, and to Leeds in the north-east, has its central pivot or key at Crewe.'

By June 1904, when an LNWR official, S. M. Phillp reflected on Crewe's further expansion in *The Railway Magazine*, it had been long established as one of Britain's great railway towns. When the Borough had celebrated its Jubilee in 1887, a lavishly produced history published by the *Crewe Guardian* noted its phenomenal growth. 'Fifty years ago the place where Crewe is now located was nothing more than a small hamlet, a few labourers' cottages scattered about, and a farm dotted here and there like currants in a penny bun for scarcity. Several of these primitive buildings still remain, though most of them are so altered as to be almost beyond recognition.'

That was because in the half century the area *had* changed beyond recognition. Clues were to be found in the nature of the Jubilee celebrations.

For as well as commemorating the 50th year of Queen Victoria's reign, the 'Rejoicings' also celebrated the 50th anniversary of the opening of the Grand Junction Railway (GJR) from Birmingham to Warrington via Crewe, the completion of the 3,000th 'engine' made in Crewe Works and the Dedication of the new Queen's Park. It was given to the town by the LNWR.

Below:
Attractively restored GJR designed houses in Dorfold Street, 1989. It was a cul-de-sac which backed on to the original Chester & Crewe main line.
Gordon Biddle

Above right:
Tait lithograph of the station about 1848 after the quadrupling of the main line. *Ian Allan collection*

Below right:
The same early station shown in Measom's *Official Illustrated Guide to the North-Western Railway* 1861. The station was completely rebuilt in 1867.
Author

The company had been created by the amalgamation on 1 January 1846 of the London & Birmingham (L&B), GJR and the Manchester & Birmingham (M&B). While the LNWR always claimed to have built Crewe, pioneering development work by the GJR deserves memory. By 1843 it had built and owned 200 'railway houses'. Many were tenanted by the 160 men already employed in the works.

The GJR moved its locomotive, carriage and wagon works from Edge Hill, Liverpool, partly because it was badly situated, being some 20 miles from the main line at Newton, later Earlestown. Not only was Crewe beside it, but land there was cheap and plentiful. Even so three years elapsed between land purchase and the move in March 1843. The Edge Hill works were beside those of the L&M from whom it rented the site, and although the move freed a large area of land the L&M never developed it. It was not until 1861 that the LNWR directors approved the large engine shed at Edge Hill

Above:
'Gaffers' Row': a restored terrace of LNWR foremen's houses in Victoria Street. They were farther away from the railway than Dorfold Street cottages. *Gordon Biddle*

Right:
The tower of Christ Church, which was built by the GJR in 1843 as part of the development of the railway town.
Gordon Biddle

which became the home of many of its Crewe built locomotives.

A striking GJR legacy at Crewe is Christ Church which lies north of the station close to the West Coast main line. It was consecrated a week before Christmas 1845, partially demolished in 1977 and reopened two years later. The stout tower remains amid new buildings including the area police headquarters, courts and library. Nearby are streets of former railway houses which have been restored in recent years. There are several types of house in the terraces, the larger ones having been the homes of foremen.

The LNWR's paternalism grew as it built schools and provided public utilities of gas, electricity and a water supply with a pumping plant beside the GJR at Whitmore.

The GJR also recruited a small police force from 1842. They were later joined by Richard Stockley as 'preserver of the peace on railway property'. He had a reputation for having used a

stout whip 'which struck terror into many lawless citizens'.

Soon a larger police force was needed for, by 1861, the population had grown to 8,159 and the LNWR's *Official Illustrated Guide* written by George Measom noted: 'The population is chiefly employed in the stations and foundries of the several railways which centre in this locality, to which circumstance Crewe owes its origin and prosperity.

'The town consists of very neat houses, appropriate to the wants and comforts of the officers and servants of the railway companies. The buildings exhibit all the resources of taste and skill in the formation of what may be called a model town. The workshops cover no less than 30 acres.'

1861 marked the start of a decade in which the population doubled to 17,810 and by the end of the Victorian age, it had passed 40,000, with most of the working population being employed by the LNWR.

It grew to be a busy rather than attractive town. A handbook for ramblers published during the World War 1 likened it to a 'soiled mechanic working hard in the middle of a grassy lawn'. But the author felt it was set in the heart of some of the finest pastoral scenery north of Dorset. For decades the LNWR could claim that the town was wholly dependent on the railway for its prosperity, but this has changed gradually. Small industries became established in Victorian days. The new industries included

numerous clothing factories, the skills of whose workers have passed from generation to generation keeping Crewe at the centre of a high quality clothing industry. One national company, Austin Reed, gives customers a card stating that clothes are made in their own factory at Crewe.

The decline of railways in the face of road competition led to Crewe losing its status as purely a railway town. Major change began in 1938 when Rolls-Royce built an aircraft engine factory to produce Merlin engines which powered Spitfire fighters. The first engine came off the assembly lines on 10 June 1939 and by 1944 the factory employed more than 10,000 people. After the return of peace, the factory switched production to luxury cars. Like the railway works, Rolls-Royce has declined in recent years and by 1988 the number of car production workers was down to just under 4,000, with further losses since then.

While industry has contracted, the size of the borough has expanded. Since local government reorganisation in 1974, it has been known as Crewe and Nantwich.

The boundary moved so far west to join Shropshire that multi-storey Rail House beside the station is reduced to Lilliputian size when you view it from distant green fields, emphasising that, whilst Crewe remains important to the railways, the railways are but a part of a much larger community — a community which has developed dramatically over the past century and a half.

3 Junctions, North and South

The lines radiating from Crewe all developed from the trunk of the GJR north-south route. None of the lines that stemmed from it was — or is — of the same strategic importance. The lines which form the North Junction are more important than those of the South Junction because they serve the Merseyside and Greater Manchester conurbations and the North Wales coast and Irish railhead at Holyhead.

The South Junction converging routes carry long distance DMU rather than InterCity services. Northwest-Cardiff Class 158 DMU services via Shrewsbury are a truncated version of the one-time Northwest-West of England expresses via the Severn Tunnel and Bristol. The North Staffordshire route to Derby survives, maintained by the longest of Crewe's all-station services.

The Grand Junction Railway

The creation of Crewe is perhaps the greatest spin-off from the concept of the Grand Junction for it had few engineering works to excite the early Victorian travellers, having none of the novelty or glamour associated with the Stockton & Darlington and Liverpool & Manchester rail-

Below:

South Junction is seen before remodelling. The work involved simplifying the track layout and eliminating reverse curves — in the middle foreground — which restricted non-stop running through the station to about 20 mph. The Diesel Depot is on the right.
London Midland Region

ways. The Grand Junction's distinguished place in history is as Britain's first trunk railway.

It was authorised on 6 May 1833 over 78 miles between Birmingham and Warrington to join the Warrington & Newton Railway (W&N), which was linked to the Liverpool & Manchester (L&M).

The GJR absorbed the W&N in 1835 so that when it opened from Birmingham on 4 July 1837, trains ran between Birmingham and Liverpool and Manchester. The first trains between London and the Northwest ran through Crewe following the opening of the London & Birmingham on 17 September 1838. A decade later the West Coast main line was completed by the Caledonian Railway (CR) opening from Carlisle to Edinburgh on 15 February 1848. It had been engineered by Joseph Locke, who had also built the GJR after initial work by George Stephenson.

An early route he surveyed passed through the historic and growing town of Nantwich four miles west of Crewe, which was the hub of the road system of South Cheshire. It was strategically situated on main roads between the Potteries, Chester and North Wales and South Cheshire, Shropshire and the mid-Wales bor-

ders. It was also a busy and well established canal centre. Why the GJR promoters avoided Nantwich and chose a direct line across the Cheshire Plain almost empty of population remains one of the mysteries of railway history.

In his classic study *The Social and Economic Development of Crewe 1780-1923*, Dr W. H. Chaloner says the most likely explanations are the opposition of Nantwich landowners and the lower price of land in purely agricultural districts as compared with urban Nantwich.

But the GJR's chosen route was not without opposition and generous compensation was paid to many local landowners.

The first station at Crewe was graded as a 'first class stopping place' despite a modest layout. It was on the north side of a bridge carrying

Below:
North Junction before the 1985 remodelling with the Manchester line to the left, the West Coast main line in the centre, the Chester line to the right and the Independent Lines on the far right. The roof of North signal box, now part of 'The Railway Age' Heritage Centre, can be seen in the bottom foreground. *London Midland Region*

the Nantwich-Sandbach turnpike much used by horse omnibuses and carriages. The station was named after Crewe Hall. Later the town took its name from the station.

Because the GJR proved so popular with passengers an unusually long time elapsed between its opening to passengers and to goods, services not being introduced until 1 February 1838. While it is generally accepted that the line was opened without ceremony for a number of reasons, including the country being in mourning for King William IV, the *Crewe Guardian* historians reported a slightly different picture. There was 'great rejoicing in the neighbourhood, and people came from all over the surrounding country to witness the strange spectacle. At various points on the line the country folk ran out of their houses to see the strange iron monster go past and wondered "what next" would be witnessed.'

GJR from Stafford to Crewe

Only small villages lie between Stafford and Crewe and the only first-class station the company built was at Whitmore (14 miles north of Stafford) and summit of the section. But it was established as a railhead, rather than simply to serve the village, a company guide noting:

'This station is fixed as an accommodation to the Potteries. The line of rail winds for nearly two miles through an excavation in solid rock ending in a kind of arch spanning the road and forming an entrance to the wild region beyond.'

That is a totally fanciful description which never fitted the quiet, green and pleasant countryside which the InterCity passenger still

Above:
'Precursor' 4-4-0 believed to be No 7 *Titan* leaving Crewe with an Up express, passing an unidentified 2-4-0. *L&GRP No 21.121*

enjoys today. The only station he passes between Stafford and Crewe is Norton Bridge (5½ miles north of Stafford), junction of the NSR branch to Stone and Stoke. It is served only by DMUs and EMUs running via Stoke. The short island platform is not used by main line trains.

Local stations had been closing since Victorian days. The first to be taken out of the timetable was Basford, which, like Coppenhall to the north, was two miles from Crewe and

Below:
The Crewe-Stafford line included a stiff climb to Whitmore. Ramsbottom 'Newton' class 2-4-0 pilots 'Claughton' 4-6-0 No 1085 on a Liverpool-Euston express. Ramsbottom invented water troughs, which were designed in Crewe works, the first being laid on the North Wales coast in 1860. For years, the LNWR supplied Crewe with water from its artesian wells around Whitmore and Madeley. *Real Photographs*

Left:
A 'George the Fifth' 4-4-0 No 5000 *Coronation* heading a Birmingham - Liverpool express on Whitmore troughs. Two horse boxes separate the locomotive from eight corridor coaches. *Real Photographs*

Above:
A heavy express climbs Basford Bank towards Whitmore in charge of No 6200 *The Princess Royal* with small, flat-sided tender piled high with coal. *Author*

Left:
'Black Five' 4-6-0 No 5409 is pictured near Betley Road with a long and heavy fitted freight. *Eric Treacy*

Left:
'Jubilee' class 4-6-0 No 45567 *South Australia* makes a spirited start past Basford Hall Junction with an Up express on Good Friday 1953. *Ian Allan Library*

close to Basford Hall Junction of today. It served a village with a paper mill, silk mill and dye-works. The station closed 1 July 1875 to make way for track improvements during Crewe-Stafford quadrupling.

The scheme was completed the following year because of traffic 'having overgrown the facilities afforded by the original two lines,' to quote an LNWR guide. At the same time a new station, Great Bridgeford (3½ miles north of Stafford), replaced a smaller one slightly closer to Stafford which the GJR had named simply Bridgeford. It survived until 8 August 1949. That was four years after the demise of Betley Road station (21 miles north of Stafford) which had been the first station south of Crewe since 1875.

Another economy after World War 2 was closure of platforms at Badnall Wharf and goods sidings at Cold Meece (eight miles north of Stafford) which had opened 3 August 1941 to serve Swynnerton Royal Ordnance Factory and a large United States Air Force base. The platforms were something of a 'back door' to both establishments which were served primarily by a branch off the Norton Bridge-Stone line and a

Below:
The Madeley Chord, nine miles south of Crewe, was opened 1962 to link the West Coast main line with the former NSR Stoke-Market Drayton branch. Merry-go-round coal train reverses in neck to right. Branch crosses the main line on the bridge in middle distance. *R. W. Miller*

four-platform terminal at Cold Meece. The branch opened two days after the platforms. Because of wartime secrecy neither appeared in public timetables.

Soon after Nationalisation, BR closed three stations on 4 February 1952: Madeley (17 miles from Stafford), Whitmore, and Standon Bridge (10 miles north of Stafford).

In the 'wild region,' beloved of the Victorian travel writer, two miles north of Whitmore, is the Madeley Chord, the only new stretch of railway built in the 'greater' Crewe area in recent years. It was opened on 18 June 1962 between the main line and the former North Staffordshire Stoke-Market Drayton branch to help electrification work by providing a route to Crewe for goods traffic from Stoke and districts to the south. That from north of Stoke continued to reach Crewe via Kidsgrove. With falling traffic, both ends of the branch closed in 1966, leaving the Chord to carry merry-go-round traffic from two collieries at Newcastle-under-Lyme. Only one remained open in 1992 — Silverdale — and this was one of a number of collieries named by British Coal and the government for immediate closure in a review of the coal industry. At the time of writing, the future of the mine is uncertain, and this must mean that the future of the remaining part of the branch is doubtful.

GJR from Crewe to Weaver Junction and Warrington

Despite the ever growing volume of traffic it was not until 1908 that the LNWR quadrupled between Crewe Coal Yard and Coppenhall Junction in work associated with the Independent Lines. The LMS extended the stretch north to Winsford in 1927. With the main line so busy,

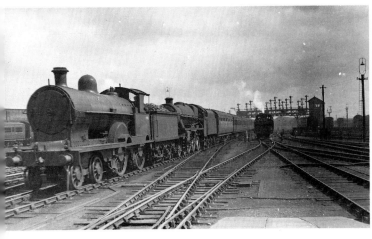

Above left:
A Euston-Liverpool/Manchester express, in July 1936, entering Crewe pulled by locomotives of two companies: ex-LNWR 'Precursor' LMS No 25212 *Harrowby* **pilots 'Jubilee' No 5581** *Bihar and Orissa.* **The tall signal box and an impressive signal gantry can be seen in the background.** *Ian Allan Library*

Left:
A month after the Manchester-Crewe 25kV electrification was officially inaugurated the old order continues: 'Pacific' No 46239 *City of Chester* **steams under the wires with a Down express, passing 'Black Five' No 45374 as it runs into the station, on 11 October 1960.** *V. Bamford.*

15

Above:

The footbridge across the north end of the station is shrouded in smoke as a double-headed express prepares to leave platform 1 in Edwardian days. 'Large Jumbo' 2-4-0 No 1173 *The Auditor* pilots a 'Prince of Wales' class 4-6-0. *Bucknall collection/IAL*

Below:

After Grouping, LNWR locomotives maintained a strong presence. 'George the Fifth' 4-4-0 No 5382 *John Rennie* arrives from the North, probably Liverpool, with a four-coach stopping train formed of compartment stock. *Paul Collins collection*

the operators were grateful that there was never a need to intensify local passenger services and it was possible, without sustained local protest, to close four of the seven stations in the 24 miles between Crewe and Warrington (Bank Quay).

Coppenhall (two miles north of Crewe) had the shortest life, closing on 10 September 1840. Minshull Vernon (five miles), built beside the Nantwich-Middlewich road, was a casualty of World War 2 — closed on 2 March 1942 — and another wartime casualty was Moore (21 miles) which shut the following winter — on 1 Febru-

Above:
The uncluttered scene in the years before electrification: Class 5MT 4-6-0 No 45446 heads a troop train 19 August 1955. Many troop trains ran through Crewe bound for Liverpool with men posted overseas. *Brian Morrison*

Right:
The North Junction maze pictured before the 1985 simplification. Visitors to 'The Railway Age' can view the modernised layout through a large observation window under the preserved signal box. *London Midland Region*

ary 1943. Its southerly neighbour, Preston Brook (18¾ miles north of Crewe), just survived LMS days, being removed from passenger timetables from 1 April 1948.

Since Minshull Vernon closed, Winsford (7½ miles) has been the first station north of Crewe. There were plans after World War 2 to make it an overspill town for Liverpool but the development never took place on the scale envisaged by the planners and today it remains a station served only by local EMU services, as is Acton Bridge (14½ miles), served only by Runcorn and Liverpool trains. It has no link with Warrington.

Until 30 June 1941 Acton Bridge was the terminus of a second, roundabout service to Crewe, operated by push-and-pull trains via Northwich and Sandbach. And until 16 June 1947 Acton Bridge was also the terminus of an infrequent push-and-pull service from Over & Wharton, terminus of a mile-long branch from the West Coast main line at Winsford Junction, opened by the LNWR on 1 June 1882. There was never a through service to Crewe, passengers having to

change at Hartford. The branch closed to revenue earning traffic on 3 October 1982 and the trackbed now awaits development.

The Beeching Report of 27 March 1963 recommended the withdrawal of local services between Crewe, Warrington, Preston and Carlisle. That was just over a year after the 18 miles of the main line between Crewe and Weaver Junction had been electrified as part of the Liverpool-Crewe work, which formed the second stage, after Manchester-Crewe, of 25kV electrification.

Crewe-Weaver Junction was the first section of the original Grand Junction line to go under

Above:
'Princess Coronation' No 46245 *City of London*, once streamlined, passes a lamp standard as it approaches a Glasgow-Euston express. The tender is still lettered 'LMS' despite this being a post-Nationalisation scene. *H. Gordon Tidey*

Below:
'Jubilee' class 4-6-0 No 45593 *Kolhapur* approaching Crewe with *The Granite City* special of the South & West Railway Society on 3 September 1966.
No 45593 was destined to be one of the last 'Jubilees' withdrawn and was subsequently preserved. *Martin Welch*

the wires. That was well over a century after it had passed into history by amalgamation 16 June 1846, six years after it had enlarged itself by taking over the Chester & Crewe.

The Chester & Crewe Railway

In 1826, a year after the Stockton & Darlington opened, George Stephenson walked through the green fields of the Cheshire Plain surveying a 20½ mile line between Chester and Crewe. Nothing came of his work and it was not until he had re-surveyed the area a decade later that the Chester & Crewe Company came into being. It was revived on the initiative of Chester and Cheshire businessmen rather than the GJR directors, who did not support such a scheme.

Stephenson considered several alternative routes, the shortest being from Chester to join the GJR at the Vale Royal Viaduct over the river Weaver near Hartford, 10 miles north of Crewe. While it would have been only 13 miles long, heavy engineering works and stiff gradients would have been needed to take it through Delamere Forest. The promoters got approval for the C&C in the first of two Acts of Parliament to which Queen Victoria gave Royal Assent after coming to the throne. The other was for the Manchester & Birmingham and both were dated 30 June 1837, four days ahead of the opening of the GJR.

One of the men involved in the construction of the C&C who was appointed soon after work

Above:
A Crewe-bound parcels train near Hartford headed by 'Jubilee' No 45553 *Canada* on 15 April 1960.
M. Mensing

began, was a young contractor, Thomas Brassey (1805-1870), who was born in the nearby village of Brown Knowl.

His rise to fame as an international railway builder started when he met George Stephenson and in 1834 he was given a contract to build Penkridge Viaduct on the GJR. Despite the flat Cheshire countryside and the need for only one

Below:
An historic locomotive in an historic setting. 'Britannia' class No 70013 *Oliver Cromwell* leaves the works on 2 February 1967 as the last steam locomotive repaired there. It stands by Chester Bridge on the original Chester & Crewe main line. The east end of the LNWR curved office block is behind the bridge. *John Hillier*

modest engineering work, a low, eight-arch viaduct over the narrow River Weaver at Worleston near Nantwich, estimates were exceeded and the C&C directors quickly ran out of money.

The GJR then bought the company under an Act of 19 May 1840 — the C&C being absorbed on 1 July 1840 never having operated a train in service — and Crewe got its first junction when the line opened on 1 October. Besides linking the towns, the C&C also opened up a second route to Merseyside over the Chester & Birkenhead which had opened only eight days before on 23 September. Two years earlier, George Stephenson had surveyed a route along the North Wales coast to Holyhead and it was this line for which the C&C was destined to be the main artery. The Chester & Holyhead (C&HR)

was authorised in 1844 but Holyhead was not reached for another six years, partly because of the time taken to build the Britannia Tubular Bridge across the Menai Strait.

Although the C&C had been an easy line to build, expansion of Crewe works led to the line running through the middle of them. Men found themselves watching locomotives which they had built passing by at the head of Chester, Holyhead and Birkenhead trains.

By the 1860s there was no land available for expansion because streets of comparatively new workers' houses had been built to the north. The last of the available land in the works was swallowed by a plant for manufacturing Bessemer steel. After new shops were opened on the south side of the Chester line the LNWR got Parlia-

mentary sanction to move the main line about a quarter of a mile to the south. An Act of 25 July 1864 provided for a deviation almost a mile long on the southern boundary of the main works.

The original line curved away from the main line a little north of the station, almost opposite the junction for Manchester and followed a shallow half-moon course.The new Chester line — the deviation — curved west far more sharply from the north end of the platforms and ran a straight course to rejoin the original route just beyond Flag Lane. It opened four years and a day after authorisation.

Meanwhile, in best LNWR tradition, nothing was wasted and the original line was adapted as an entrance to the works. Distinctive general offices were built in almost a parkland setting on the north side of the original line. After they opened in 1876 they became an imposing and favoured backdrop to many of the company's official photographs of staff groups, locomotives and distinguished visitors.

In a sense the new Chester line still ran through the works, though not the centre, for as the works grew to be among the biggest in the world, land on the south side of the deviation was developed, carriage repair works covering several acres on a site dominated by the LNWR's own gas works. The carriage works were closed by the LMS in 1932, but the gas works remained in railway ownership until the gas industry was nationalised in 1952.

Crewe's 'Ghost' Station

When BR began building Crewe Locomotive Works Training School on part of the carriage works site in 1951, a recruiting brochure stated that there was a station alongside with that title

on a name board. The station was, in fact, a platform built in 1926 as the terminus of trains from Stoke and other parts of the Potteries. They were introduced to carry men to the works after the LMS closed the Stoke locomotive works of the North Staffordshire Railway, which it had absorbed only three years before. The platform — or halt — did not close until 24 April 1989 but for more than 60 years it remained a 'ghost' station since it never appeared in public timetables.

The Crewe works area and sidings south of the Chester line were linked to the main works by Eagle Bridge carrying a single track across the Chester line which found its way into *LMS Route Book No 1: The Track of the Irish Mail* because it was flanked by large metal eagles. They were delivered to Crewe as scrap metal in Victorian times, reputedly from an old bridge at Conwy in North Wales, and saved on the orders of F. W. Webb, the Chief Mechanical Engineer, who happened to see them awaiting destruction.

When Eagle Bridge was demolished the eagles found champions for a second time. One guards the works entrance in West Street. Another keeps an eagle eye on Crewe North Junction from an eyrie above the flat concrete roof of the old signal box now imaginatively incorporated into 'The Railway Age'. Another is at the entrance.

Opposite, across the Chester line, is the single storey Crewe Signalling Centre, hardly distinguishable from adjacent modern warehouses, but its site is historic for it lies on land once crammed by locomotives stabled at Crewe North Shed (code 5A). All had to use the C&C to enter or leave: a cramped bottleneck to a cramped site. Today the C&C still provides access to a locomotive shed: the Electric Traction Depot also built

on part of the site of the carriage works during the main line electrification.

The complex incorporates Crewe Electric Control Room covering an extensive network of lines and, until its closure in 1991 for conversion to Metrolink, the Manchester Victoria-Bury 1,200V system.

The Chester line was electrified for more than 1½ miles from Crewe station to a short distance beyond Steelworks box. An electrified shunt-back from this stretch provides the only rail access to the works and nearer the station, a second shunt back leads into 'The Railway Age'.

Chester & Crewe: Local Stations

It is now more than a quarter of a century since the clunk-clunk of date stamping ticket machines could be heard at a string of five almost evenly distanced little stations between Chester and Crewe. Almost 14 years elapsed between closure of the first — Worleston (3¾ miles) and the nearest to Crewe — on 1 September 1952, and the last, Beeston Castle & Tarporley (10¾ miles from Crewe) on 18 April 1966. This was the busiest of the intermediate stations and the only one still open when the Beeching Report recommended its closure together with the withdrawal of Chester-Crewe local services. Tattenhall Road (14½ miles from Crewe), closed to passengers on the same day.

Above:
The Manchester & Birmingham approach to Crewe was sharply curved. A corridor express passes the tall signal box which dominated the Junction until it was replaced in 1906. The Spider Bridge connecting the station with the North shed and the Works is visible to the left. *Bucknall collection/IAL*

Its neighbour, Waverton (18 miles from Crewe), within sight of Chester, had closed on 15 June 1959 and Calveley (8¼ miles from Crewe), and closest to it since Worleston closed, on 7 March 1960. (See Appendix 2)

Three stations had undergone name changes in Victorian days. Worleston was called Nantwich until 1 September 1858. Tattenhall Road was originally called Crow's Nest and Waverton was Black Dog. Waverton was rebuilt in distinctive style by the Duke of Westminster in 1887.

The Manchester & Birmingham Railway

While the Chester & Crewe linked the places named in its title, the M&B got no further south than Crewe and for its entire life was effectively the Manchester & Crewe. Yet as the historian Herbert Rake noted in *The Railway Magazine* for June 1905 'the Manchester & Birmingham, oth-

Above:
North Junction is viewed c1870 with LNWR four and six-wheel coaches and vans in sight. The works lie on the north side of the Manchester line. *L&GRP*

erwise the "Manchester & Crewe" line played a part in the railway world far transcending its proportionate mileage.'

The M&B was the only one of the companies meeting at Crewe which was strongly opposed, the GJR fearing loss of traffic from a rival London-Manchester route. The M&B was born of agitation in the early 1830s by Manchester merchants who wanted a shorter route to Birmingham than that via the Liverpool & Manchester and GJR via Warrington. A line of no more than 30 miles between Manchester and Crewe would reduce the overall distance from 99 miles to 82. Such a saving was highly attractive, both in mileage costs and speed.

But the merchants were divided and two rival schemes were promoted, both of which angered the GJR directors. The Manchester & Cheshire Junction promoters proposed a line direct to Crewe to link up with the Grand Junction and the C&C which they saw as the springboard for a major route to Holyhead for Irish traffic.

The strategy of the Manchester South Union was different, their proposal being for a line from Manchester through Macclesfield and the Potteries to the Birmingham & Derby Junction line at Tamworth totally independent of the GJR. From Tamworth there was to be a branch to the London & Birmingham at Rugby to provide a shorter Manchester-London direct route.

The Cheshire Junction promoters quickly changed the emphasis of their plans by project-ing a line from Alderley (later Alderley Edge) via Congleton and the Potteries to the GJR at Chebsey, a village north of Stafford. It lies about a mile west of Norton Bridge, where the North Staffordshire Railway (NSR) later joined the LNWR with a branch from Stone. When the South Union and Cheshire Junction schemes went before Parliament in 1837, the idea of two railway lines running almost parallel through Staffordshire failed to impress MPs and their promoters then agreed a compromise.

As a result the Manchester & Birmingham Railway, which was authorised on 30 June 1837, provided for a main line from Manchester via Alderley, Congleton and the Potteries to Chebsey. There was to be a branch to Crewe from Alderley, 13½ miles from Manchester London Road and 17 miles from Crewe.

Another branch, from Stockport to Macclesfield, later linked up with the NSR main line through Stoke completing the route by which many Euston-Manchester and Manchester-Birmingham services avoid Crewe. Even though the authorised M&B of 1837 ended miles north of Birmingham, it was further truncated by an Act of 1839 which provided for the branch from Alderley to Crewe to become part of the main line, making Crewe the only junc-

Right:
A Bowen Cooke superheater 4-6-2 tank, LMS No 6996, heads an express of GWR coaches c1929. *Paul Collins collection*

Below right:
'Jubilee' No 45686 *St Vincent* heads a troop train on to the Up main line passing a 'Patriot'class 4-6-0 on a parcels train (right background) making for a platform track. Pictured on 1 June 1956, this was another typical scene of the pre-electrification era. *S. D. Wainwright*

Below:
The Sandbach-Northwich branch was a diversionary route which was particularly useful during electrification work. The down Sunday 'Mancunian' is caught about to cross the Trent and Mersey Canal near Middlewich headed by 'Royal Scot' No 46143 *The South Staffordshire Regiment* on 15 April 1956. *T.K. Widd*

tion with the GJR. The Act also allowed alteration of the route between Congleton and the Potteries but this was later abandoned.

Another three years elapsed before Manchester and Crewe were linked by the opening of the last section of the M&B — the 4½-mile stretch between Sandbach and Crewe on 10 August 1842. It had been delayed for three months because of a bitter dispute with the GJR which contested the M&B's right to run its own trains between Crewe and Birmingham. The victor was the GJR which agreed to work Manchester trains over its metals taking 70% of the receipts, charging the M&B for 38 miles instead of 54.

Initial through working at Crewe was primitive. The M&B had its own platform outside the GJR station, which was connected by a single line controlled by a gate which had to be opened for every train that passed. The first were passenger services between Manchester and Birmingham and also Chester.

The gate was a boundary between track gauges as well as companies because the M&B rails were 4ft 9in apart, the extra half-inch being considered useful to give wheels extra 'play.' It was a third gauge at Crewe for the Chester line was laid to 4ft 8¾in for the same reason.

Crewe became more than a grand junction of the gauges because the M&B completed the Crewe North surface junctions. They were formed of lines soon to be swallowed by the LNWR. Less than a decade had passed since the authorisation of the GJR and the arrival of the

first train from Manchester. It was a tremendous achievement.

The M&B got increased traffic following the opening by the LNWR of its Sandbach-Northwich branch, to goods on 11 November 1867 and passengers from 1 July 1868. It survives as a useful diversionary route between Crewe and Manchester, having been reprieved in 1992 after plans were announced to close the northern section between Middlewich and Northwich. It has been Sandbach's only junction since the closure, in 1971, of the single former NSR branch from Lawton Junction, Alsager. It opened in 1866 and in recent years formed, with the Northwich branch, a route by which some freight trains could avoid Crewe.

The NSR line junction was at the northern end of the 4½ miles between Crewe and Sandbach which the LNWR got powers to quadruple on 4 August 1890. The quadrupling was completed on 1 July 1895. It was a project associated with construction of the Independent Lines, which joined the route at Sydney Bridge Junction. It had involved building a second viaduct alongside Elton viaduct over the River Wheelock. The LMS had to replace it with an

Below:
Sandbach, the first station north of Crewe on the Manchester line, was among those rebuilt for electrification in September 1960. Nine months earlier, Sandbach lost its second passenger service with the withdrawal of Crewe-Northwich motor trains. *London Midland Region*

embankment in the 1930s because of severe subsidence problems in this brine-pumping district.

Today severe speed restrictions remain in force over much of the section because of continuing subsidence problems and since electrification, in 1960, tracks have been kept level by layers of large concrete pipes underpinning a steel deck. Overhead wires are kept tensioned by adjustable cross-supports. The embankment restrictions remain a handicap to BR's hopes of two-hour Euston-Manchester services.

The quadrupling did not significantly alter the layout of the M&B's sharp curves at the approach to North Junction. That was not

Above:

The NSR took coal from local pits to Crewe over its own metals. NSR Class E 0-6-0 No 106 passes Radway Green with a train from Sideway on 29 July 1912. The engine was 60 years old when it was scrapped by the LMS in 1932. It is interesting to note both Up and Down line signals on the same tall signal post. *Ken Nunn collection LCGB*

Below:

Empty coal wagons from Crewe returning to the Potteries passing Radway Green. The train is headed by NSR 0-6-2T Class L No 157 on 29 July 1912. The locomotive was one of a class of 16 built between 1908 and 1913 at the NSR's Stoke Works. It survived until February 1936, when it was withdrawn by the LMS. *Ken Nunn collection LCGB*

achieved until the 1985 modernisation and although the layout was simplified and the curves eased, it is still severely speed restricted, although Manchester line expresses not stopping at Crewe can approach and depart faster from North Junction on the realigned middle roads through the station.

Above:
The Loop line, linking the Crewe-Kidsgrove line with Basford Hall marshalling yard, was de-electrified and singled before closure on 1 October 1984. Two unidentified Class 25s make use of the line on 28 April 1984. The West Coast main line bridge, on the left, is close to milepost 157^1/4. *Gordon Biddle*

The North Staffordshire Railway: Crewe-Kidsgrove

The GWR reached Crewe only by exercising running powers and today its presence is recalled only by historians. But the former North Staffordshire Railway (NSR) retains a physical presence because of its 8½-mile line from Kidsgrove, which forms part of an artery between the West Coast main line and Eastern England.

Crewe-Kidsgrove was the northern tip of one of the NSR's main lines authorised in the company's original Acts of 26 June 1846 — a line of 14½ miles from Stoke-on-Trent to Crewe to join the LNWR (a company which was formed on 16 July in the same year). The LNWR saw it as rather less important, describing it in its public guides as 'a short branch line constructed to accommodate the salt traffic of Cheshire'. Once authorised, the NSR wanted the branch opened

as soon as possible and employed more than 500 navvies. They were held up by delays in acquiring land from Lord Crewe. Delays became so prolonged and bitter that the NSR was forced to obtain an Act in summer 1847 for a deviation of over three miles from Crewe South Junction to Radway Green.

After the route opened on 6 October 1848 traffic was slow to develop. This was partly because of disagreements with Euston. They lasted for a number of years and the NSR took some to the Queen's Bench Division for a legal solution.

It was not until 1859 that *Bradshaw's Shareholders' Guide* reported a new arrangement 'by which it is expected that all the disputes with the LNWR may be amicably arranged and traffic renewed'. A decade later the NSR built a small locomotive shed just short of the main line at Crewe and also a coal yard at Cumberland Wharf on the West Coast main line nearly a mile north of the station. The yard has closed but the signal box which controlled it, Crewe Coal Yard, remains open.

While still a main line in the sense that it carries a Crewe-East Midlands passenger service, the Kidsgrove line declined after World War 2 when passenger traffic had reached a peak with hundreds of workers travelling between the Potteries and factories at Crewe. Special trains ran day and night to match workers' shift patterns.

Some traffic was lost because the route was not electrified. As early as 1961 the then Transport Minister, Ernest Marples, told the House of Commons that there were never plans to do so. Freight traffic decline led to the closure in 1962 of North Staffordshire Down sidings and the transfer of marshalling to the newly electrified Basford Hall yard. In 1984 the Stoke Goods Loops which the LNWR had built into the Yard were closed because of further loss of traffic. The Loops, as the LNWR termed them, formed a double track which burrowed under the main line just south of the Carriage Sheds on the Up side and ran parallel to Basford Hall Junction.

The junction was close to the neck of the yard and although NSR traffic had to reverse before being sorted, the Loops were heavily used for many years.

Hopes that Crewe-Kidsgrove might go 'under the wires' were revived when *Railnews* reported in 1984 that the London Midland Region (LMR) was preparing a case for electrification so that InterCity expresses could call at both Crewe and Stoke and local EMU services between Liverpool, Manchester and Crewe could be extended to Stoke. There was little support for the proposal and it was abandoned. Crewe-Radway Green has been singled, the only such economy on the six routes that meet at Crewe.

Some goods traffic to and from the Potteries ran through Crewe station for many years even after the opening of the Independent Lines and the Kidsgrove route was valuable to the NSR as the outlet from which it could use running powers for goods traffic to Liverpool, direct via Runcorn and through Warrington, and to Mold Junction.

Crewe-Stoke has lost two stations — Chatterley on 27 September 1948 and Radway Green & Barthomley on 7 November 1966 — and Radway Green Royal Ordnance Factory platform has also disappeared, being closed in 1959. But it has been possible since 1989 to book to and from Crewe from a reopened station, Tutbury & Hatton. This is the only station to be reopened in recent years on lines used by Crewe stopping train services; the station had originally closed on 7 November 1966.

The Shrewsbury & Crewe Railway

Like the Chester & Crewe, the Shrewsbury & Crewe was built as a through route for Wales rather than as a line local in concept serving only scattered small towns and villages.

Below:
A Crewe-bound freight crosses the Trent & Mersey Canal just south of Kidsgrove station hauled by ex-LMS 'Crab' No 42888 on 26 September 1960.
M. Mensing

Left:
The NSR tradition of long trains of empties continued through the LMS years and well into Nationalisation. 'Crab' No 42885 leaves the Crewe line at Kidsgrove Central station on 26 September 1960. *M. Mensing*

Below left:
Streamline glory: an unidentified, new and shining 'Princess Coronation' is pictured at Gresty Lane Junction with a West-North express of GWR stock. The spur to Basford Hall yard and the Independent Lines can be seen to the left. *Nigel Payton*

Below:
A Liverpool/Manchester-West of England express in July 1951, formed of LMS stock, approaches Nantwich with Longsight-shedded Class 5MT No 44749, fitted with Caprotti valve gear, providing the motive power. *Eric Treacy*

Right:

A Shrewsbury & Crewe running-in turn: 'Princess Royal' class No 46202 *Princess Anne*, which had been rebuilt from the 'Turbomotive', is about to back on to the 10.40am Crewe-Shrewsbury train on 23 August 1952. Just over six weeks later, on 8 October, the locomotive was destroyed in the Harrow & Wealdstone disaster. The disaster led to expresses being temporarily diverted to Paddington via Nantwich and Wellington. *W. H. Whitworth*

Below right:

Class 158s maintain most Northwest-Cardiff services after displacing locomotive-hauled stock. Class 47 No 47199 stops at Nantwich with the 16.00 Crewe-Cardiff on 8 July 1978. *E. A. J. Saunders*

The S&C was the only one of the Crewe lines to be built by the LNWR alone. The 32½ mile line was authorised on 20 August 1853 as part of the LNWR's strong territorial ambitions to reach Mid Wales by supporting Welsh promoters building lines to the Cambrian Coast and through Central Wales.

The S&C was the only important line to be built in Shropshire during the 1850s. It was engineered through gently rolling countryside by Joseph Locke and J. E. Errington and took the railway to the heart of Nantwich which until then had an inconveniently sited station on the Chester & Crewe line two miles to the north. That station was renamed Worleston on the opening of the S&C on 1 September 1858.

Construction of the line had taken several years because of a dispute about the approach to Shrewsbury. It was single track and described as a 'branch' in Measom's *Official Illustrated Guide to the North-Western* of 1861. But that concept changed when it was doubled the following year to handle ever increasing traffic.

Some of it was due to the the opening in summer 1864 of the Oswestry, Ellesmere &

Whitchurch Railway (OE&W) which completed the Cambrian Railways main line to Cardigan Bay. Crewe became a place where passengers changed for Whitchurch to catch Cambrian Railways trains to the Cambrian Coast.

The strategic importance and value of the S&C improved dramatically with the opening of the Severn Tunnel in 1886. It enabled the LNWR and GWR to break the Midland's monopoly of West of England services via Birmingham and Bristol. Services between the West of England, the North and Scotland were soon introduced with locomotive changing taking place at Shrewsbury. The GWR handled traffic south of the town; the LNWR to the north. Most of the S&C ran through countryside and it was only in the Crewe area that there was any potential for the development of passenger traffic. The LNWR opened two Motor Halts. Gresty, serving Gresty Green, was about 1¼ miles from the main line station. It lay just west of where running lines and sidings funnelled into the double tracks of the S&C. Newcastle Crossing Halt was between Willaston and Nantwich. The Halts were shown without suffixes in LNWR timeta-

bles. Some sources state that they closed on 1 April 1918, but this may have been temporary for they are shown in Bradshaw's July 1922 timetables. Willaston station survived until 6 December 1954.

Although the closure of other stations and the withdrawal of local passenger trains was recommended in the Beeching Report, they have stayed open. However, Prees and Yorton village stations were downgraded to request stops in 1992.

More than a mile of the Shrewsbury line in the vicinity of Gresty Lane yard was electrified under the West Coast project and in May 1961 the short section took on a pioneering role when extra equipment was brought into use so that a restricted electrically hauled freight service could be introduced to Manchester. This was at a time when electric passenger services, begun the previous September, were still running in steam timings.

The GWR at Crewe

Nantwich, an LNWR station, was served by GWR passenger and goods trains running through to Crewe over its secondary main line from Wellington to Nantwich. They joined the S&C half a mile west of Nantwich at a junction supervised by the station master. GWR Service Time Table Appendices laid down that guards of goods trains must show junction passing times in their journals.

The GWR reached Crewe in 1863 after completion of the first section of the 10¾ miles GWR backed Nantwich & Market Drayton Railway (N&MDR) on 20 October. Trains were headed by small locomotives shedded at Market Drayton. The N&MDR formed the first section of the 27½-mile secondary route between Wellington and Nantwich, which was completed by the Wellington & Drayton Railway on 16 October 1867. The GWR used powers under an 1863

Above left:
In 1992 single railcars replaced two-car sets on Crewe-Shrewsbury stopping services. Two and a half decades earlier, on 13 June 1967, the station at Nantwich still possessed wide platform canopies and a partly glass-screened lattice footbridge and gas lighting. *Andrew Muckley*

Above right:
Some DMU services have been extended over long distances bringing new travel opportunities. On 6 February 1982, the 07.50 Aberystwyth-Crewe service calls at Nantwich on the last lap of its 114 mile journey. Coach No M56503 leads the Class 142 unit. *Bill Chapman*

Below:
The GWR secondary line from Wellington brought a variety of that company's locomotives to Crewe. 'Manor' class 4-6-0 No 7809 *Childrey Manor* departs 'under the wires' with the 7.50pm to Whitchurch on 29 June 1959. *Ian Allan Library*

Above:
Many Crewe-Wellington stopping trains were in charge of ex-GWR 2-6-2 tanks. No 4120 pauses at Market Drayton with the 12.52pm from Crewe on 4 August 1959. *P. J. Shoesmith*

Above right:
The GWR presence at Crewe ebbed away in two stages. Wellington passenger services were withdrawn on 9 September 1963 but the line remained open until goods services were withdrawn on 1 May 1967 when it was closed completely. Several weeks later, Market Drayton station and its signal box looked virtually intact. Point rodding, signal wires and gas lamps were still *in situ*. *Andrew Muckley*

agreement to run over the S&C into Crewe Station, 31 miles and 68 chains from Wellington (Market Drayton Junction).

The agreement also provided for the LNWR to handle GWR passenger and goods trains at Nantwich, and for LNWR passengers to use the GWR trains between Nantwich and Crewe. The value to the GWR of access to Crewe was not so much in being able to develop passenger traffic, but rather as a goods artery. This was reflected in the organisation of the 33 staff employed at

Crewe under a Yard Master. Most worked for the goods department, an internal company report stating that the Yard Master 'supervises the work in connection with GWR trains at the passenger station'. It added that the greater portion of his time was spent at Gresty Lane Sidings.

The GWR presence at Crewe was swept away during the period of electrification: the Wellington local service being withdrawn on 9 September 1963 and Nantwich-Wellington closed completely on 1 May 1967.

Despite the agreement for GWR access to Crewe, the LNWR used the S&C as a weapon to try to break the GWR's monopoly of goods traffic between Shrewsbury and Chester by building a 15-mile branch from Whitchurch to Tattenhall Junction on the Chester & Crewe, opened on 1 October 1872, it did not prove an intensively used alternative route, but it did reduce some of the LNWR's growing goods congestion problems at Crewe which were not eased until Basford Hall yard was reconstructed.

Below:
Another of the GWR's sturdy and distinctive 2-4-0s: No 3234 awaits to leave the south end of Crewe station. *R. E. Priestley*

4 Station

'This is Crewe...Crewe Station...Crewe.' Passengers hearing for the first time the station announcer's stentorian delivery of the time-honoured phrase and then seeing the station, might have been disappointed in not finding one far grander for so important a junction. But the only thing that the LNWR never built at Crewe was a station to be a jewel in the crown of a railway-created town. Instead, from the modest, almost primitive adjacent stations of the Grand Junction and Manchester & Birmingham companies grew a station which was extended as passenger traffic expanded.

Crewe station remained purely functional rather than ornate because nothing more was ever needed. It is still a place travellers pass through rather than begin or end their journeys. There was never a need for a stylish station like

Below:
The primitive station of 1843, six years after the GJR opened and only a short time after the Manchester & Birmingham's completion. The station scene was to change out of recognition a few years later. *Author's collection*

those in historic cities like York, Chester, Carlisle and Bristol.

The first station, opened by the Grand Junction Railway, was a relatively small scale affair, although designated 'first-class'. All trains stopped there for coach connections to Sandbach and Nantwich. A small, single engine, loco shed was also provided. Also built at this time was the Crewe Arms Hotel built by Lord Crewe. This remained in private ownership until 1864, when the railway took a 40-year lease at £225 per annum. The railway bought the hotel in 1877.

An enlarged two-platform station appeared with the opening of the Chester & Crewe line in 1840. The C&C had been absorbed by the GJR (on 1 July) three months prior to opening. It was this station that the LNWR inherited.

The first major improvements were made as the LNWR was formed in order to accommodate the extra traffic generated from the opening of the line through Lancaster and Carlisle to Scotland, and the increase in traffic on the Chester and Crewe routes. The new station, illustrated by Tait in 1849, retained two platforms but had

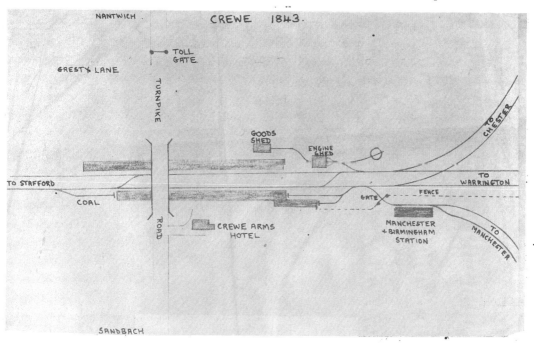

Above:
A view south from North Junction in LNWR days gives a good idea of how cramped was so busy a junction. A saddle tank shunts close to the horse landing (left) while a small 2 4 0 locomotive waits under the shadow of Spider Bridge to back on to an express. *Jim Peden Collection*

the addition of two through running lines in the centre. The new company used the existing station and junction layout for some 20 years until 1867. It was impressive — 'A very handsome building in the Elizabethan style,' to quote *Measom's Guide*, 1861 edition. *Black's Picturesque Tourist and Road and Railway Guide Book* noted that it had 'extensive waiting and refreshment rooms with every convenience for the accommodation for passengers'. It was in Crewe station in 1861 that the first ever application of Bessemer steel rail was attempted; prior to that date the iron roads had lived up to their name.

This was replaced by a more spacious station from 1867. Platforms were widened and given bays so that local trains and other services stopping at Crewe could be kept clear of the main line. The next major improvements came a few years later with the building of more platforms and a station entrance to replace one in a 'dip' near the Crewe Arms Hotel. It opened — on the site of that of today — in 1878.

With expansion came a big increase in staff. When Thomas Humphries moved from Bletchley to become stationmaster at Crewe on 12 May 1875 he took charge of about 150 men. That number had doubled by the time he retired through ill health in 1898. He had held what was described as 'a position of enormous responsibility'. He often met the Prime Minister, Mr Gladstone, as he changed during journeys between his home at Hawarden, near Chester, and London. He was also thanked by Queen Victoria.

He also received — and was allowed by the LNWR to accept — lavish gifts such as those from the Empress of Austria who after hunting in Cheshire for several seasons, presented him with a ring set with diamonds and rubies. He was born of an age when stationmasters were held in great respect and awe and after his death a road past the side of the Crewe Arms Hotel to the horse landing (later the short-lived motorail terminal) was named Tommy's Lane.

Humphries was never an Army officer like so many senior railway officials, but he was born into an Army family, his father having served under the Duke of Wellington. A retired officer still remembered as a notable stationmaster from 1933-1949 was Major C. J. Cowley, whose authority was also supreme within station limits, as he demonstrated when the LMS spent thousands of pounds installing a public address system. He decreed that, despite the expenditure, the only trains to be announced were those running late. He ordered staff to stop broadcasting announcement after announcement. This is in dramatic contrast to the contemporary scene where, today, BR customers are advised that while there is a duty station manager, the sta-

Left:
The pre-electrification station frontage was strongly North Western in style. The decking of Nantwich Road — the original turnpike — was supported by thick steel girders. It was replaced during electrification because of the need for bigger clearances. In the autumn of 1992 severe weight restrictions were placed on the 1960 bridge and it awaits rebuilding. On 19 August 1955, 'Royal Scot' 4-6-0 No 46164 *The Artist's Rifleman* departs with a Merseyside boat express: 'The Empress Voyager' from Euston to Liverpool Riverside with passengers for a Canadian Pacific liner. Special bogie van (for bullion?) behind locomotive. *Brian Morrison*

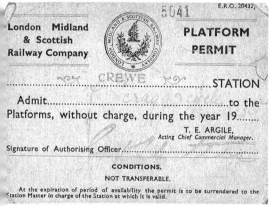

Above:
The LMS issued free platform tickets to staff. This example, for Mr H. Scragg, included his cycle and was valid for the whole of 1939. *Author's collection*

tion is the responsibility of the InterCity Retail Manager. He is based at Liverpool.

Years of Change

Twice in this century, Crewe station has undergone major modernisation. In 1903-06 (as the Independent Lines were being constructed), it was virtually doubled in size by the addition of a third island platform. This work involved the demolition of the house constructed more than 60 years earlier for the first stationmaster Capt Winby. For years the LNWR boasted about Crewe platform lengths, stating in *The Railway Year Book* that faces which trains could go alongside totalled 11,361ft. No 1 Down platform was 1,509ft 'probably the longest in the world'. It was, of course, a totally unjustifiable claim.

North Staffordshire trains from Derby and GWR services from Wellington ran into south bay platforms. Both companies kept small staffs at Crewe to handle their services. The GWR's accommodation consisted of a rented booking office, passenger agent's office, lamp and porters' rooms.

Improvements of LMS days included a facelift for the entrance and a centralised booking office which replaced those on platforms Nos 1, 4 and 5. The work was carried out shortly before World War 2.

When dense locomotive smoke was trapped under eight acres of glass roof the atmosphere could be gloomy but there were welcome improvements with the building of two footbridges and a subway to help passengers and staff and postal workers to get about. In this form the station existed for more than three decades. The war years brought tremendous traffic pressures and especially when trains were changing locomotives or making scheduled stops, soldiers, sailors and airmen rushed to the Coffee Tavern on platform No 3, owned by the station staff, and temporary wooden-hutted canteens. They were staffed by volunteers, the canteens served tea cheaper than the station buffets in thick china mugs and such charity was

Left:
Because of its cramped position on the Nantwich Road overbridge, it was impossible to give so famous a junction station a striking new appearance during electrification. The carriageway behind the glass screen is just wide enough for two cars to squeeze through. *Ian Allan*

Below left:
Because of engine changing during electrification, the station was often crowded with locomotives and stock. The Friday before August Bank Holiday, 1961, with blue liveried electric locomotive No E3020 about to depart with a Euston-Manchester express. English Electric No D325 in foreground has just arrived with a Euston express and a new four-coach EMU destined for Liverpool-Crewe local services which began the following January, is in the far platform. *B. A. Haresnape*

extended to penniless loco spotters, as I found in the mid-war years. They closed soon after the war ended, although they were still remembered by the time electrification once again brought major change.

While Euston, Birmingham New Street, Manchester London Road (Piccadilly) and Stafford stations were rebuilt, Crewe got little more than a face lift. The level of Nantwich Road bridge was raised to give electrical clearances and the station forecourt and booking hall rebuilt.

Station Manager's Organisation

Some of the most far reaching changes of recent years have been in staffing with large reductions and alterations in manning patterns to match those of train services.

The winter 1960 timetable brought a seasonal reduction in services but Crewe station was still busy, handling 181 Down passenger and 41 parcel trains; 155 Up passenger and 27 parcel trains, with 24 freight trains booked to pass through the station.

The stationmaster had a deputy and three assistants, 19 inspectors, 35 foremen, 53 shunters, 104 parcel porters, 44 other porters and 20 ticket collectors. In addition to those staff concerned with train operation and parcels handling, there were train ticket collectors, train reporters, letter sorters, train announcers, carriage servicemen, office cleaners and junior porters.

The operating and parcel staff duties also covered two yards adjacent to the station used for the shunting and marshalling of parcel trains and stabling some coaching stock. The Down yard, the original goods marshalling yard, had 12 sidings and was so busy that a shunting engine was almost continuously at work.

Uphill Sidings, as the other yard was known, was a group of 10 close to North Junction. They ran alongside the Up Manchester line and a connection was put in as late as 1960.

A major and historic administrative change took place on 9 January 1967 when a Station Manager replaced the time-honoured post of Stationmaster.

The Manager's duties reflected the complexities of operation of the station in an era when an average of 400 trains a day were still being handled and the pattern of services had been radically revised after electrification.

The Station Manager was responsible to the Divisional Manager for the operation of passenger and parcel trains using the station; local motive power involving the control of train crews and locomotives; booking and parcel offices and the telegraph office and telephone exchange, the control of carriage and wagon examiners and of the carriage shed, where trains were cleaned.

An Assistant Station Manager, (Station), a title which would have been better designated as ASM (Operations), was responsible for movements and working. He had a supervisory staff of 37 responsible for the work of 500 'wages grade' staff. They included signalmen, yard and station foremen, shunters, train reporters, ticket collectors, train announcers, leading parcels and senior parcel porters, domestic porters, letter sorters, juniors, passenger guards and train ticket collectors.

A second ASM (Motive Power) had charge of 28 supervisors of about 1,200 'wages grade' staff, mainly footplate crews. The Station Manager also had an Administrative Assistant responsible for clerical work 'at various points in the Organisation, approximately 106 units', including the main booking office.

Modernisation 1984-1985

'I offer my warm congratulations to the 1,200 people who formed the round - the - clock team that took to pieces the most famous railway junction in the world at Crewe and put it together again in seven weeks.'

This was British Rail chairman, Sir Bob Reid's, tribute in *Railnews* after the £14.3 million track and signal modernisation of the mid 1980s. It was the second major upheaval in recent years and had an impact on the station far greater than the main line electrification of the 1960s (see Chapter 6).

Below:
The scene after modernisation: the midday 'Manchester Pullman' behind No 86254 accelerates on the Up Fast 'middle road' which it joined over the improved junction between the Manchester and West Coast lines at North Junction on 27 July 1985. The waiting room known to generations of passengers, was remodelled as part of the 1985 modernisation and renamed 'Passenger Lounge'. *Colin Boocock*

Below right:
During the seven week long shutdown, only the old platform 1 was serviceable. It was used by a Chester-Crewe DMU shuttle. A similiar service operated between a temporary platform at Crewe and Stafford. *Dr L. A. Nixon*

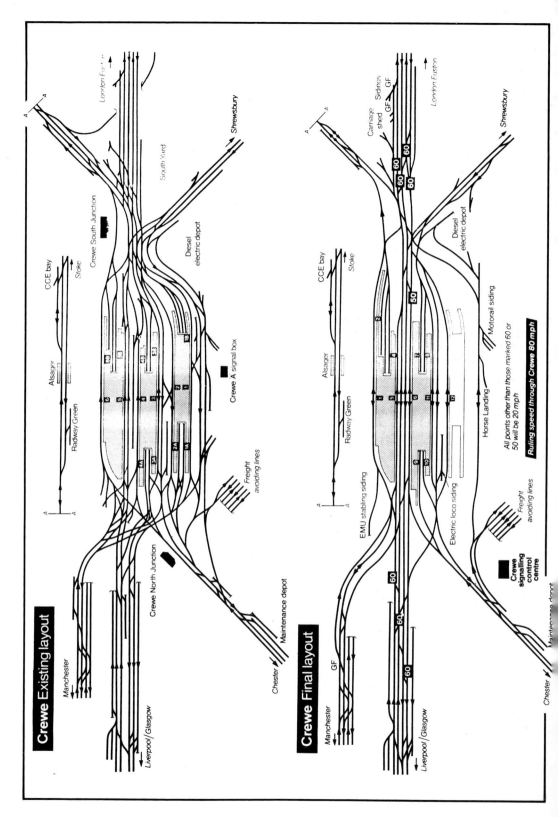

Crewe Existing layout

Manchester
Liverpool / Glasgow
Chester
Maintenance depot

CCE bay
Alsager
Radway Green
Stoke

Crewe North Junction

London Euston
South Yard
Crewe South Junction
Diesel electric depot
Shrewsbury

Freight avoiding lines

Crewe 'A' signal box

Crewe Final layout

Manchester
GF
Liverpool / Glasgow
Chester
Maintenance depot

CCE bay
Alsager
Radway Green
Stoke

EMU stabling siding

Electric loco siding
Horse Landing
Motorail siding
Freight avoiding lines

Carriage shed   Sidings
GF   GF
London Euston
Diesel electric depot
Shrewsbury

60   60
60   60
50
60
60
60

All points other than those marked 60 or
50 will be 20 mph

Ruling speed through Crewe 80 mph

Crewe signalling control centre

It was carried out under the greatest glare of nationwide publicity Crewe had ever known, as the travelling public were kept informed of service changes during the virtual shutdown of the station from 2 June to 21 July 1985. That was the period when the public were most aware of the scale of the modernisation though it was in progress for some two years, mainly with resignalling work. The shutdown was considered the best way of reducing inconvenience to passengers and BR estimated that it saved nearly £1 million which would have been spent if the work had been done in stages taking up to four years to complete.

Points and crossings were reduced from 285 to 110 and the biggest change was the closing of all but the eastern face of the most western of the three island platforms, the last to be added in the 1900s. Track was ripped up from platform No 1 and the double track bays at either end of platforms Nos 1 and 2. Platform No 2 is now platform No 12 but it is not open all the time, being used only as traffic demands.

Among work carried out before the shutdown was the reconstruction of the booking hall and the building of a travel centre adjacent. They were officially opened on 2 February 1984 by the Mayor of Crewe and Nantwich, Councillor Roy Billington, a BREL plater.

In the modernised station of summer 1985, passengers found renovated waiting rooms and buffets and toilets, goods lifts to platforms Nos 5 and 6 near the ticket barriers converted for passenger use (and much used) and nearly 50 information display screens.

Some platforms were lengthened and ramps replaced lifts to subways to improve the operation of Post Office trolleys. Only Platform No 5 retained its original number and it was here on 22 July 1985 that Crewe and Nantwich MP, the Hon Gwyneth Dunwoody, unveiled a commemorative plaque to mark the completion of modernisation. The occasion had a sense of history for the plaque was sited above a drinking fountain installed in 1863 'for ye dogs'.

Today platform No 12 becomes a place of nostalgia when preserved 'Princess Royal' class Pacifics and other veteran steam locomotives work North Wales and Shrewsbury excursions. To use the platform they run under 25 kV installations strengthened at the expense of Crewe &

Nantwich Borough Council in 1987 to encourage tourists to visit the town and Heritage Centre. The sight of the veterans momentarily time warps a station which, despite radical improvement, has changed little in overall character. The retention of comparatively low glass roofs, LNWR brick retaining walls and glass screens preserves an air of cosiness.

Crossing the southern footbridge between Crewe's two island platforms still takes you almost into the roof support girders and is rather like climbing into a loft. But its not something most changing passengers often experience because Crewe is a station where cross-platform, rather than over-the-bridge, connections are made by operators exploiting the flexibility of the remodelled layout. Also the northern footbridge is more popular because of its lifts.

The most unusual approach to the station was through a 'covered way' under the Nantwich Road between the station and the Crewe Arms Hotel — a feature stressed in hotel advertisements. The LNWR leased the hotel from Lord Crewe in 1864 and bought it in 1877, the directors stating: 'A well managed and comfortable hotel at such a centre as Crewe, the hub of the system, was thought to be a necessity.' Hotel porters in red coats met all principal trains and intending guests could telegraph for rooms free of charge from LNWR or Caledonian Railway stations by telling either stationmasters or the guard on their train. Enthusiasts have been known to book their honeymoon accommodation at the hotel — making sure their room overlooked the railway!

Above:
An advertisement for the Crewe Arms Hotel in the LNWR timetables noted that it adjoined Crewe station 'where trains connect with every part of Great Britain'. In October 1915 the hotel telephone number was Crewe 21. The timetable warned that, because of wartime conditions, some Euston-Northwest expresses would run to earlier timings and the daily Northwest-Bournemouth service was discontinued. *Author's collection*

5 Independent Lines and Basford Hall Marshalling Yard

Historians generally regard Crewe as the most complete railway town in Britain. Unlike Swindon, its nearest rival for the title, it is not only a company-built town with houses, public buildings and utilities, a large station and a major locomotive building works, Crewe also has an extensive marshalling yard at Basford Hall, south of the station.

The labyrinth of lines reached their zenith in Edwardian days with the building of the goods lines to keep trains clear of the congested station, and in and out of the yard. This was greatly extended at the same time over land between Shavington and Crewe which the Company had bought in 1873 as congestion first became acute.

All the works were needed because the LNWR could no longer cope with the volume of passenger and goods traffic generated by its own success. By 1894, 1,000 trains a day were passing through the Crewe junctions. Many reached them by running over main lines which had been widened progressively or provided with loops for some years as company policy.

The 'Big Dig', as the Independent Lines construction work was known locally, began in 1896 and took several years. On 5 August 1901, the LNWR engineer reported: 'About 46 miles of additional lines and sidings are now available for goods and mineral traffic'.

The Independent Lines stretch for some 2½ miles from Basford Hall Junction 1¾ miles south of the station to Coal Yard and Sydney Bridge junctions. At the hub is Salop Goods Junction signal box where several routes meet. The box is in a shallow cutting close to a double track north-facing spur, opened about 1899, connecting the Liverpool and Manchester lines with the Shrewsbury & Crewe route at Gresty Lane No 1 box. A south-facing spur from the box takes traffic to and from Basford Hall Yard.

Of the three pairs of lines which pass the box, the Liverpool and Manchester lines burrow

Below:
The generous layout of the Independent Lines was the result of foresight by the Grand Junction and LNWR in buying land in early Victorian years for expansion not envisaged until decades later. A train load of Halewood-manufactured Ford vans headed by No 85021 approaches Salop Goods Junction at the heart of the Basford Hall complex. It formed the 12.37 from Garston Speke Junction Sidings to Maidenhead on 30 June 1975. Rail House is in background. *David Clough*

under the station and the Chester line runs in a 415yd tunnel, but they make slightly different approaches to the tunnels.

The Up Liverpool line descends from Coal Yard box to burrow under the main line while the Down Liverpool climbs to reach it. The Up and Down Manchester tracks burrow from Sydney Bridge Junction. They opened on 24 March 1901. Because of the position of the locomotive works, the LNWR could not carry the Independent Lines across the North Junctions on flyovers and the work did not quite relieve the station layout of all conflicting traffic.

Passenger and goods trains between the Stoke branch and Chester still had to run through the station, although the LNWR kept most NSR goods traffic, including that to Liverpool, clear with a double tracked Loop burrowing under the main line. (Page 27).

Basford Hall Marshalling Yard

The enlarged yard had a capacity of 2,350 wagons covering two groups of sorting sidings. Their layout reflected traffic flows for the Down group could handle 1,600 wagons, more than double the total of its neighbour. Each had their own reception and dispatch lines and necks.

There was a Tranship shed, a project pioneered by the LNWR in summer 1901 as a new method of sorting small consignments of cross-country traffic carried by goods train. Soon after it opened, more than 600 men handled a daily average of 600 arriving wagons. They loaded 500 more with over 20,000 packages. The success of the operation led to other companies opening similiar sheds. The building survives, but in other use.

Further expansion of the Yard took place in 1928 with the opening of Gresty Lane Down Sidings, a mile from the station on the Down side of the Shrewsbury line. At the same time the 14 Basford Hall Up sidings were lengthened and six more laid. By the 1930s the yard was claimed as Europe's busiest, handling more than 400 trains a day and 47,000 wagons a week.

Basford Hall was made up of nine independent yards which in 1960 had a total of 96 sidings with a capacity of 5,394 wagons. The layout consisted of Basford Hall Sorting Sidings South, simply a group of six reception roads; BH Sorting Sidings Middle, with 20 sidings on the Up side, 30 on the Down; Gresty Lane Down Sidings (18 sidings plus two arrival roads), Gresty Lane Down two sidings; Gresty Green eight; Gresty Lane (ex-GWR) five; North Staffordshire Up four and NS Down, nine sidings.

The 1960 staff complement of the yard totalled 439. It included 168 goods guards and 80 shunters.

The run-down of the yard to its present day layout dates from the Beeching years which rid BR of loose-coupled trains. In the early 1960s the yard was electrified and remodelled. Thirty-three single track miles embracing part of the Independent Lines, reception and departure lines and entrances to groups of sidings were wired.

Left:
The 09.09 Birmingham-Llandudno, which is not booked to stop at Crewe, is signal-checked beside the Red Star parcel office (left) before taking the single track Chester Independent Line. The train is headed by Class 47 No 47556 and the date is 6 July 1985.
A. Sherratt

Above:
The Independent Lines proved valuable during the 1985 modernisation. A Stafford-Crewe shuttle service DMU on the Down Slow Independent Line passes Sorting Sidings Middle box on 8 July. *J. Winkle*

Below:
A busy scene during the same period: a Bangor-Northampton parcels train headed by Class 25 No 25206 has just passed under the Shrewsbury line, and is about to be overtaken by the 'Merseyside Pullman' headed by No 86240 *Bishop Eric Treacy* on 24 June 1985. *Paul Biggs*

A new hump to improve shunting was built and the Down sidings remodelled. The work began in October 1961 and the first electrically-hauled commercial freight services were introduced from 18 June 1962.

The Crewe-Glasgow electrification brought fresh traffic and in 1973 the author travelled in the cab of the first electrically-hauled transfer freight from Warrington Arpley yard to the Up reception lines at the south end of Basford Hall. It was a trip memorable for weather as well as railway history for I made the long trek back to the station in a thunderstorm!

Almost a decade later the yard was run-down with long distance freight transferred to Bescot and Arpley, but revival came in 1982 after Freightliner began using sidings at Basford Hall and today the yard is a focal point in its traffic. Trains run in and out of a slimmed down yard in which many sidings have been lifted and two signal boxes closed.

A fan of parcel van sidings occupies the site of Crewe South steam shed. It is partly shielded from the main line by trees which, as they grow, give an increasingly rural air to the old yard. Despite being so close to Crewe and the station, much of the yard is in the country with cows grazing beside the boundary fence. The yard is renowned for its wild life including foxes, which show little fear of man's presence.

Retired railwaymen still remember the nicknames of sidings. Among those which got official recognition was 'Pan Mug'. For years the man in charge had to telephone the Control Room at 6 o'clock every morning 'or at commencement of work' to report traffic or coaching stock stabled there.

Across the main line on the Up side just south of North Staffordshire Junction is a seven-road brick carriage shed also dating from early 1900. It had an LNWR stated capacity of 147 vehicles and it is still a depot for electric multiple units and Class 158 diesel trains, but is never crowded with stock.

It lies between the Kidsgrove line and the cutting in which the Stoke goods loops burrowed under the main line. It demonstrated how the LNWR used every piece of available land as it did on the west side of the Independent Lines cutting. Sidings from the Shrewsbury line at Gresty Lane No 1 signal box served a large stores building, timber yard and Crewe cattle market, established through LNWR initiative to attract traffic.

The shunting neck of the two sidings of the timber yard continued behind Crewe Alexandra Football ground and a spare open wagon was often left in the neck as a railway workers' grandstand for home matches.

6 25kV Electrification and Signalling

'Change at Crewe...It's all Change at Crewe. And what a change! From steam to electricity.' The excitement of the completion of the Manchester-Crewe electrification was caught in the introduction to a glossy, coffee table book published by the London Midland Region.

The LMR said it was 'the first step in their bold and ambitious plan for complete modernisation'. The pilot scheme of 42 route miles and 144 single track miles included conversion of the Manchester South Junction & Altrincham between Manchester Piccadilly and Oxford Road stations.

The British Transport Commission announced its plans for main line overhead electrification at 25kV single-phase ac on 6 March 1956. On the LMR, the first three stages, centred on Crewe, were for the Manchester, Liverpool and Birmingham routes. The first two routes were completed as planned but Crewe-Birmingham was one of the last links to be forged.

Although Crewe-Liverpool conversion would have involved less major reconstruction work, the Manchester line was completed first because the single track Sandbach-Northwich branch was a useful diversionary route, especially as it was directly linked to Manchester Central, as well as London Road station. Despite the diversions, it retained its infrequent service of Crewe-Northwich local trains until 4 January 1960.

These services were shown in *Bradshaw's* as running between Manchester Central, Northwich and Crewe, while, in fact, they connected at Northwich with Chester trains over the

Below:
Before electrification masts ensnared North Junction skies above were clear of clutter! The 1955 scene as a Glasgow-Birmingham express arrives behind 'Pacific' No 46235 *City of Birmingham* — one of the de-streamlined 'Princess Coronations', easily identified by a sloping, firebox front. The North Box is in the middle distance. The date is 19 August 1955. *Brian Morrison*

Right:
Crewe-Manchester electrification: the masts are in position at Sandbach on 5 April 1959. The DMU was working a shuttle service between Sandbach (and its rebuilt platforms) and Crewe to connect with some diverted services. Sandbach Power Box was built on part of the Goods Yard on the Up side, which was not closed completely until 6 February 1967. *F. L. Marsland*

Below right:
'Caprotti' Class 5 No 44686 departing from Chelford with the 6.30pm Manchester London Road-Crewe, all stations, is framed between partly completed electrification masts on 1 May 1958. *T.K.Widd*

Below:
During the first Easter after Manchester-Crewe conversion, electric traction takes over the 9.15am Paignton-Manchester Piccadilly on Good Friday, 31 March 1961. The train is headed by No E3031.
M. Mensing

Cheshire Lines Committee route. Their withdrawal produced the irony of the new Sandbach power box overlooking the junction of a branch which had recently lost its regular passenger service.

A diversionary route even more useful was the Styal line, between Slade Lane Junction, Longsight, and Wilmslow, which also provided an ideal test track as I found soon after it was electrified from 26 October 1958. I spent a night recording a programme for BBC Radio 3 on a test train shuttling at between 5 mph and 100 mph track testing with scientists from Derby.

Once the Styal line was wired, construction teams moved south of Wilmslow and test trains were running to Sandbach by October 1959.

The Manchester-Crewe electrification was officially inaugurated by a West of England express signalled away from Manchester London Road station by the then Minister of Transport, Ernest Marples, on 12 September 1960. He had also renamed the station Manchester Piccadilly.

The new timetable was temporary, with electric traction running according to the previous steam timings. Four days earlier, I experienced line speeds which had been well beyond the capabilities of the steam engine. Leaving Crewe in the cab of blue electric locomotive No E3025 on a press train made up of five first-class dining cars, we broke the 'magic' 100 mph speed barrier, reaching 102 mph near Jodrell Bank radio telescope, another recent symbol of Britain's latest technology.

One of the biggest projects of the early years of electrification was conversion work at Crewe, which involved more than 70 miles of tracks within a mile radius of the station.

An electric traction depot incorporating a supply control room was built on the site of old carriage sidings on the south side of the Chester line and a construction material storage depot was also established there.

Special sidings were laid at Crewe to reduce time taken to locomotive changing from either diesel or steam to electric. It was a problem that intensified after a full and accelerated Manchester service was introduced in June 1961, and again when Crewe-Weaver Junction-Liverpool Lime Street electric services began on 1 January 1962. Trains ran according to steam timings until 18 June. West Coast main line services continued with diesel or steam traction.

The date 18 June 1962 was also significant for it marked completion of the next stage — electrification of Basford Hall yard.

Another major development of 1962 concerned conductor wire clearances. After extensive tests on flash-over distances including some in the Crewe Independent Line tunnels, the Transport Minister allowed reduction by three inches. It led to savings estimated at a million pounds in the London-Northwest project by eliminating a large amount of engineering work which would have been necessary to provide the original clearances.

Below:
A Manchester-Plymouth express, doubled-headed by Nos E3047 and E3009, is pictured approaching Crewe. The leading vehicle is a Gresley luggage van.
Ian Allan Library

Locomotive changing at Crewe began to ease as electrification was extended by four additional sections, each of them shorter than the Crewe-Manchester and Crewe-Liverpool schemes: Crewe-Stafford (24½ miles), 7 January 1963; Lichfield (17¼ miles), 22 October 1963; Nuneaton (19¼ miles), 2 March 1964; Rugby (14½ miles), 16 November 1964. As these stretches opened, traction changing was carried out at each place until through running between Euston and Manchester and Liverpool began with electrification between Euston and Rugby on 6 November 1965.

In an *Advice to Drivers* leaflet, the LMR stated: '3 January 1966 marks the culmination of seven years of intensive construction work on the electrification of the Euston-Manchester-Liverpool line.'

It continued: 'Successful operation of the accelerated electric services, by which we expect to win much additional revenue, depends on drivers utilising the power reserves of the ac electric locomotives to the full in maintaining the timings laid down.'

But all was not complete. Crewe and Birmingham passenger services were not electrically hauled until 6 December 1966 after the Rugby-Birmingham New Street-Stafford route and other lines in the West Midlands had been energised in stages during 1966. The Euston-West Midlands-Northwest scheme of 412 route miles was completed on 6 March 1967 with the intro-

Above:
More than two years elapsed between the Manchester-Crewe conversion and the extension of electrification to Stafford. On 12 September 1960, the day Manchester-Crewe electric services began officially, an electrification contractor's train from Stafford to Crewe climbs Madeley Bank on the Down Fast line. It is headed by 'Jinty' 0-6-0T No 47458. There are no signs here of impending conversion work and the line is still flanked by tall telegraph poles. *Derek Cross*

duction of a totally new pattern of electrified services. Crewe continued to be a locomotive changing frontier for North Wales expresses and Birmingham-Glasgow services were diesel-hauled until completion of the Weaver Junction-Glasgow electrification on which work began in 1971.

Changing continued longer than planned because of the postponement of electric services between Crewe and Preston. A Special Supplement to the 1973 summer timetable starting from 7 May stated the delay was 'for reasons outside the control of British Rail'.

Through running began from 23 July when Warrington and Wigan were also electrically linked with Crewe and the Capital. Less than a year later, on 7 May 1974, the Queen visited Preston to inaugurate the 'Electric Scots' services through to Glasgow introduced the previous day. Fewer trains now stopped at Crewe because Euston-Glasgow expresses ran non-stop to Preston.

Left:
Locomotive changing at Crewe lasted longer than planned because electrification to Preston was delayed for nearly three months. The full service was not introduced until 23 July 1973. *Author's collection*

SPECIAL SUPPLEMENT
to
LONDON MIDLAND
PASSENGER TIMETABLE
Dated 7 May 1973 to 5 May 1974

DELAY TO THE INTRODUCTION
OF ELECTRIFIED WORKING
BETWEEN CREWE AND PRESTON
COMMENCING 7 MAY 1973 UNTIL
FURTHER NOTICE

For reasons outside the control of British Rail, it will not be possible to complete the electrification to Preston in time for the commencement of the new timetable from 7 May 1973.

The date for the introduction of electrified working to Preston will be announced as soon as possible, but during the interim period this special supplement to the London Midland Region Passenger Timetable will apply. (See important note on page 2)

When electrified working Crewe to Preston commences this special supplement should be destroyed. From that date the service times shown in the timetable will apply.

Signalling

Visitors to Crewe North signalbox preserved in 'The Railway Age' get sweeping views of the junction which signalmen knew for years. Privileged visitors to the Signaling Centre have only a small window from which to glimpse expresses rushing through. In the 1985 modernisation, the Centre replaced six boxes of great individuality.

North and South and the former LNWR 'A' cabin (now in the Heritage Centre), were closed together with three of the NSR boxes, which dated from 1880: Radway Green, Alsager station and Alsager East. Level crossings at Radway Green and Alsager station passed to closed circuit television control at the Centre. Kidsgrove, controlling entry and exit to the Crewe line, is a

Above right:
Crewe Station A cabin, closed on 15 July 1985 during modernisation, is open again — as a visitor attraction at 'The Railway Age' Heritage Centre. *Author*

Right:
Crewe Signalling Centre under construction in June 1984 on the site of the North locomotive sheds. *J. Winkle*

Below:
North Junction signal box portrayed in *The Official Tourists' Picturesque Guide to the LNWR*, published in 1876. *Author's collection*

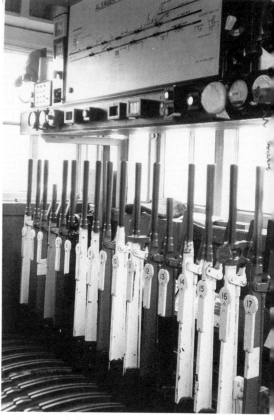

Above:
Crewe Station A cabin was equipped with a Webb Thompson frame. *J. Winkle*

Right:
Alsager Station box was closed on 3 June 1985 under the modernisation programme. *J. Winkle*

Below:
The box seen in the middle distance across the Chester & Crewe line, in figure 9. It has tall, narrow windows rather than the square ones of its companion box. *Author's collection*

fringe box together with Basford Hall Junction, Salop Goods Junction, Gresty Lane, Crewe Steel Works and Crewe Coal Yard and Sandbach.

Several boxes were closed ahead of modernisation including North Staffordshire Sidings. An earlier closure had been a box at Barthomley, which was opened only for Stoke Wakes holidays.

The LNWR was acclaimed for its signalling. It began making its own equipment in 1874 using parts of the works including the old tender shop between the original Chester line and the deviation. A decade later a large signalling shop was opened at the northern end of the steelworks. It later became the brass foundry.

The signal, telegraph and electrical departments were combined on 1 July 1903 and the following year the new department moved to new works in Gresty Lane. In 1905 the telegraph works moved from Stockport, the vacated site

being used for carriage sheds. A further move came in 1966 when the signal works were transferred to the west end of the old locomotive works in Richard Moon Street.

Large signalboxes added character to the station scene. The most notable were those at North Junction. One built in 1878 had 144 manual levers and was claimed to be among the biggest in Britain. It was in use until 1906 when manual signalling was replaced by a system of all-electric point and signal operation adopted by Webb and Thompson, the company's electrical engineer. It followed a practice which was becoming increasingly popular in America and, as Richard D. Foster noted in *A Pictorial Record of LNWR Signalling*, the company was considerably ahead of the times in adopting an all-electric form of signalling. The scale and complexity of the work remained unequalled in pre-Grouping days.

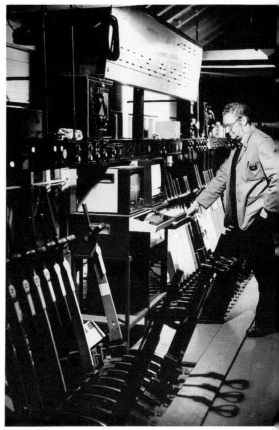

Above:
Gresty Lane on the Shrewsbury line is a busy fringe box to the Signalling Centre. *J. Winkle*

Right:
Another important fringe box is Basford Hall Junction, in which old and new technologies work side by side. *J. Winkle*

Below:
Until 1906 North Junction was dominated by a three storey box on the north side of the Chester line beside Spider Bridge. *Jim Peden Collection*

Facing page, top:
The three storey cabin was replaced by a cabin built at right angles around the end of Spider Bridge. The works tramway passed through it at mid level. *Jim Peden Collection*

North box was equally innovative in design being built round 'midge bridge' carrying a branch of the works 18in tramway to the north end of the station on a long, slender suspension bridge over the Chester line. The tramway ran through the box. Tramway use ceased in 1932 but the bridge survived until 1939, carrying pedestrian and light rubber-wheel works trollies.

The LNWR built nine cabins, as they were popularly termed, during the 1899-1906 modernisation. They controlled about 1,000 points and signals. Those in the station — neat and squat A and B had flat roofs to fit under that of the station. One of the main attractions of electrical signalling was that the system was labour saving with only two men a shift needed to easily work the largest installations.

In summer 1940 — during the Battle of Britain — the LMS replaced North and South boxes with two having distinctive and ugly flat roofs of reinforced concrete as a protection against bombing. Both had frames of small levers. Those preserved in North box, which was commissioned on 25 August 1940, have been adapted as a working exhibit.

South box, now an empty shell, was built into a low embankment opposite the box of 1900. During construction water caused landslip and several lines had to be closed for a short time until the land could be stabilised.

The boxes remained in operation until 1985 because, while the Manchester line needed resignalling for main line electrification, only limited modifications to meet high voltage were needed to the Crewe signalling system.

Sandbach was Britain's first electronic power signalbox and incorporated Sydney Bridge, among the first of BR's remotely controlled junctions. A then-revolutionary system linked box and junction, nearly four miles away, by only two wires instead of thousands needed for a conventional system.

Sandbach box is a large double storey glasshouse structure dominating the station, the four tracked main line from Crewe and the junction of the Northwich branch.

In contrast, Crewe Signalling Centre is housed in a single-storey off-the-peg industrial warehouse building. the Crewe resignalling and modernisation did not achieve an operator's dream of high speed junctions not least because of a shortage of land on which to lay more generous turn outs. But it enabled the fast line speeds to be raised from 20-30mph to 80mph and trains stopping to approach at 50mph. The panel allows the selection of 645 routes and bi-directional platform working gives a flexibility for connecting services to use adjacent platforms.

When Basford Hall yard was modernised in 1961-62, two new boxes were opened — Sorting Sidings Middle Up and Sorting Sidings Middle Down — and Sorting Sidings North box was modernised. They were fitted with illuminated diagrams and switch panels made a short distance away in the Gresty Road workshops.

Accidents

Although there have been many serious accidents on the West Coast main line at Weaver Junction and Winsford north of Crewe, there have been none close to the station, mainly because of expresses travelling slowly under severe speed restrictions.

Twenty people were slightly hurt when an overnight express from Perth ran into the back of one from Glasgow as it was starting from Crewe Coal Yard box. That happened on 16 November 1937.

Below:
After the multi-million pound modernisation of 1985, men in the new Signalling Centre worked a high-speed layout with points and crossings reduced from 285 to 110. *Author's collection*

Earlier the same year, a coach on the Down daytime 'Irish Mail' mounted a platform and hit the station roof as an axle broke as it was coming to a stand. Several passengers were shaken; a young railwayman who went into the wreckage to retrieve a passenger's briefcase got a tip worth almost his weekly wages.

This was not the first time an accident of this kind had happened. In late Victorian times, a down night Scotch express ran into one of the south bays, smashed through the buffers and reared up onto a platform. No one was seriously hurt.

It is not known if anyone was disciplined but over the years a number of the GWR men — and no doubt others — based at Crewe were cautioned for misdemeanours and these examples provide a fascinating picture of the nature of railway operation in the pre-Grouping era. In 1893 a head shunter was found guilty of causing damage to a brake van and wagons by leaving a wagon foul of a siding. In 1898, a porter was suspended for three days after Cambrian Railways' van No 253 was damaged during shunting.

A Crewe-based goods guard was suspended for three days without pay for not taking proper rest at Worcester on 8 July 1899 and returning to duty late to work the 9.50pm from Worcester to Crewe. A GWR Manchester based guard was severely reprimanded and cautioned for not examining the condition of sheep in a truck in his train and drawing attention to their condition.

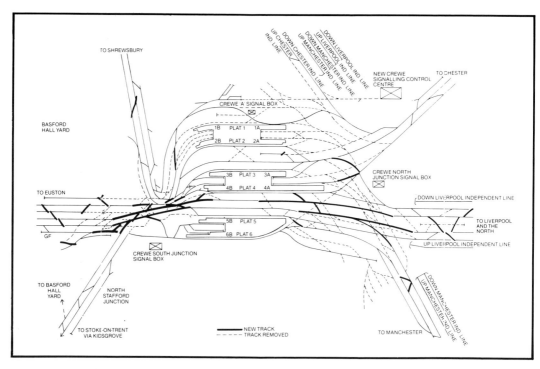

7 Passenger Services

For decades passenger trains of infinite variety delighted spotters who crowded a footbridge which spanned the track maze of North Junction. None was more memorable than the 'Coronation Scot' which ran for only two years up to the start of World War 2. None was more obscure than the motor trains which ran between Crewe and Northwich in the same era, with their small tank engines 'leading to Northwich'.

There has never been a major accident at Crewe yet 'the accident that almost was' is still talked about by veterans more than half a century later. Harold Forster still remembers standing on the south end of platform No 3 on 29 June 1937 waiting for the streamlined Pacific No 6220 *Coronation* to complete a press run from Euston with the 'Coronation Scot' express.

In the distance he saw it pass Basford Wood Box at 'such a high speed that it frightened the life out of me. I turned and ran back down the platform - and was still running when it came to a stop in the station.'

It had — just — negotiated three successive cross overs at high speed as it slowed from 113mph at which it was running only two miles to the south of the station.

Crockery and pans went flying in the dining car but as one of the timekeepers, Cecil J. Allen, recorded in *The Railway Magazine*, there were 'no worse casualties than a few unexpected embraces of passengers preparing to alight'.

Another veteran Crewe railway officer, Nigel Payton, remembered more than half a century later that as a fellow inspector was giving him a training walk round Basford Hall yard, 'the special shot past Sorting Sidings South in a cloud of dust. My companion offered thanks that no free tickets were allowed on the demonstration run!'

Two days earlier the London & North Eastern Railway (LNER) 'Silver Jubilee' streamlined express had made high speed runs as the LMS & LNER battled for supremacy for Anglo-Scottish traffic over the West and East Coast main lines, while Crewe-built Pacifics of the 'Princess Royal' and 'Princess Coronation' classes provided the cream of the motive power for the most famous of LMS expresses.

Not all of them stopped at Crewe, but all had to observe the 20mph speed restriction which so

Below:
Starting a second historic run: LMS Streamlined 'Pacific' No 6220 *Coronation* departs from Crewe with the return 'Coronation Scot' press special on 29 June 1937. It reached Euston in 119min — 16min ahead of schedule — after what Cecil J. Allen, one of the time recorders, described as an 'extraordinary performance'. *Nigel Payton*

bedevilled West Coast main line high speed running until 1985. It was only a mile or two faster than the average speeds of the first trains to arrive when the Grand Junction Railway opened in 1837.

Early Passenger Services

The inaugural service, when the Grand Junction opened in 1837, was of four first-class and two mixed trains a day which ran between a temporary terminus at Vauxhall, Birmingham, and Liverpool and Manchester via Newton Junction in about 4½hr northbound and about an hour longer southbound. All stopped at Crewe because it was a first-class station. Departures from Crewe northbound were 9.24am (first), 11.29am (mixed), 1.54pm (first), 4.54pm (first),

7.29pm (mixed) and 9.24pm (first). In the southbound direction departures were at 8.32am (first), 10.53am (mixed), 1.32pm (first), 4.32pm (first), 6.53pm (mixed) and 8.32pm (first). A similar pattern of six services was maintained the next year, although times were altered to give earlier departures both north and southbound.

The growth of Crewe as a junction led to widespread congestion on the main line and the speed of trains improved only as major improvements in track and signalling were made. The LNWR directors noted in 1876 that before Crewe-Stafford was quadrupled 'this section had been responsible for many delays'.

Among the longest distance expresses passing through Crewe are those between Euston and Scotland to Edinburgh, Glasgow and Inverness. 'The Royal Scot' has a notable pedigree dating from the Victorian 10am 'Scotch Express' which in 1885 was allowed 3hr 41min including stops

No. 5. — To Birmingham and London.

From Bank Quay.	Week Days.													Sundays.		
	1,2,	1,2,3,	1 & 2	1 & 2	1,2,	1,2,		1,2,	1 & 2	1,2,3,	x			1,2,	1,2,3,	x
Warrington	4 54	8 30	9 38	11 10	12 2	2 0	...	4 14	5 38	6 48	11 30	..	..	4 54	10 25	11 30
Moore (arrival)	..	8 41	..	..	..	..		..	..	7 2	..	..		..	..	..
Preston Brook..	..	8 52	..	..	..	2 20	...	..	...	7 14	..	..		...	..	..
Acton..........	..	9 3	..	..	..	2 30	...	..	...	7 23	..	..		...	...	..
Hartford	..	9 13	10 1	..	12 33	2 39	...	..	6 0	7 30	..	...		...	10 50	...
Winsford	..	9 25	..	..	..	2 50	...	..	..	7 40	..	..		...	...	...
Minshull Vernon	..	9 33	..	..	..	...		..	..	7 48	..	...		...	...	...
Crewe..........	5 34	9 45	10 20	11 50	1 0	3 5	...	4 55	6 20	8 0	12 15	..	5 34	11 10	11 57
Stafford	6 20	11 45	11 0	..	2 15	4 5	...	5 48	7 10	9 15	1 10	...	6 20	12 5	1 0
Birmingham ..	7 50	1 20	12 20	1 35	3 30	5 30	...	7 5	8 15	10 50	2 0	...	7 55	1 35	2 6
Rugby	8 20	2 4	12 28	2 42	5 12	7 30	...	7 8	8 33	—	3 5	...	8 20	2 0	2 56
London.......	11 0	6 0	2 30	5 0	8 20	10 40	...	9 15	10 50	..	5 20	..	11 0	6 15	5 20

(The Classes refer to London and Warrington only.)

No. 6. — From London and Birmingham.

	Week Days.														Sundays.		
	1,2	1,2,3	1,2,	1,2,	1,2,3	1,2	1,2.	1, 2	1,2,	1,2,	x	x			1,2,3	1,2.	
London (dep,)	..	..	6 15	6 30	7 30	9 0	10 0	..	1 0	2 45	5 0	9 15	..	..	8 0	10 0	9 15	..
Rugby	..	..	8 25	10 0	11 25	11 0	12 40	..	4 30	4 45	7 0	11 10	..	..	1 0	12 40	11 4	..
Birmingham....	..	6 0	8 45	10 15	...	11 10	1 15	..	4 50	5 0	7 15	10 40	..	..	1245	12 45	11 50	..
Stafford	..	7 0	10 0	12 0	2 0	12 24	2 37	..	6 14	6 3	8 15	12 39	..	..	3 30	2 25	12 28	..
Crewe	6 0	8 20	10 40	12 50	3 30	1 1	3 25	..	6 50	6 58	9 10	1 22	..	...	4 5	3 20	1 11	..
Minshull Vernon	6 9	8 32	..	..	3 45	..	..		..	..	..	..	..	4 20	..	..	..
Winsford [wich	6 14	8 40	...	1 24	3 52	..	..	8 22	..	..	..	..	4 27	..	..	..
Hartford & North-	6 23	8 50	11 2	1 33	4 3	..	3 47	5 10	8 31	7 15	..	..	..	4 38	3 40	..	..
Acton	6 32	8 58	..	1 42	4 13	..	..	5 18	8 38	..	..	..	..	4 48	..	..	..
Preston Brook..	6 43	9 9	..	1 52	4 24	..	..	5 27	8 47	..	..	..	..	4 58	..	..	..
Moore	6 49	9 18	..	..	4 30	..	..	5 33	8 53	..	..	..	..	5 5	..	..	..
Warrington ..	7 0	9 25	11 25	2 7	4 40	1 43	4 10	5 50	9 5	7 35	9 50	2 20	..	..	5 15	4 8	2 20	..

Above:
Third-class passengers were carried on only two of the trains shown in *The Warrington Guardian* broadsheet timetable for May 1860. It showed Hartford station as 'Hartford and Northwich'.
Author's collection

Below:
Easter relief to the Up 'Royal Scot' approaching Hartford headed by No 46252 *City of Leicester*. The train reporting number — W 96 — is chalked across the smokebox. The locomotive chimney is hidden by black, billowing smoke. The date is Good Friday 15 April 1960. *M.Mensing*

at Willesden Junction and Rugby. After stopping at Crewe for 6min for an engine change (an operation which added so much interest and fascination to the station scene for the whole of the golden days of steam), the express departed for a 1hr 5min run to Preston.

Here there was a further stop of 25min 'for Passengers to dine', stated *Bradshaw's Guide*. Preston had bigger refreshment rooms than Crewe and was closer in distance and time to the half-way mark of many Anglo-Scottish journeys.

Titled trains of which the 'Royal Scot' remains Crewe's most famous, are only birds of passage on the junction scene. If they stop they do so only to make connections for passengers, not to serve the town.

Crack expresses generally had the unusual distinction of being among the few trains handled at Crewe that were neither split nor broken there, either by having coaches and vans added, or portions or individual coaches removed.

In 1933 the 'Royal Scot' followed different seasonal schedules, which were shown in a publicity booklet called *The Triumph of the Royal Scot* to commemorate its North American tour. In summer, the express ran non-stop between Euston and Carlisle, where it stopped for engine change. But in winter there was a three-minute stop at Crewe made 2hr 57min after Euston departure. The schedule from Stafford was eased by 5min compared with the summer timings to allow for a slower approach to Crewe.

The Up service did not stop at Crewe summer or winter. Apart from the 1937 test run, the 'Coronation Scot' was never scheduled to call, but in two short years until the outbreak of World War 2, it brought glamour and two unusual liveries to the West Coast main line.

It also gave birth to the 'streamliner' age at Crewe in which the blue livery and horizontal white bands of the streamlined casings fitted to several Pacifics for working it, was continued on the tender and the sets of specially adapted standard LMS coaches.

The entire train was not streamlined like 'The Silver Jubilee'. When a more luxurious set of coaches was built for the 'Coronation Scot' service in 1939, the livery was changed to standard LMS red with the horizontal lines in gold.

The train was among the shortest lived that appeared on the 'passing' Crewe scene. Another, after World War 2, was the 'Caledonian' introduced between Euston and Glasgow to polish

THE TRACK OF THE ROYAL SCOT—*Continued*

THE UP TRAIN

	Miles	Winter Schedule		Summer Schedule	
Penrith	118¾	Pass	12.38 p.m.	Pass	12.35 p.m.
—*Shap Summit, 915 ft. above sea level*—					
Summit	132¼	Pass	1.0	Pass	12.56
Oxenholme	150½	Pass	1.18	Pass	1.14
Carnforth	163¾	Pass	1.30	Pass	1.26
—*Our only glimpse of the Sea is at Hest Bank*—					
Lancaster	170	Pass	1.36	Pass	1.32
PRESTON	191	Pass	1.59	Pass	1.55
WIGAN..	206	Pass	2.19	Pass	2.14
Warrington	217¾	Pass	2.27	Pass	2.22
—*Between Warrington and Moore, we cross first the River Mersey and then the Manchester Ship Canal*—					
CREWE	242	Pass	2.59	Pass	2.52
—*L M S Locomotive Works at Crewe cover 165 acres*—					
—*There is a stiff climb from Crewe to Whitmore*—					
Whitmore	252½	Pass	3.13	Pass	3.6
STAFFORD ..	267½	Pass	3.27	Pass	3.20
—*The great Queensville Curve, beyond Stafford*—					
Lichfield.. ..	283¾	Pass	3.45	Pass	3.38
Nuneaton	303	Pass	4.4	Pass	3.57
RUGBY	317½	Pass	4.20	Pass	4.13
—*Kilsby Tunnel, 2,400 yards in length*—					
Blisworth	337	Pass	4.40	Pass	4.33
—*Roade Cutting, 1½ Miles long, Maximum Depth 70 ft.*—					
Roade	339¾	Pass	4.43	Pass	4.36
—*Wolverton Works, Birthplace of L M S Carriages*—					
Bletchley	353¼	Pass	4.55	Pass	4.48
—*15 Miles climb to crest of Chiltern Hills at Tring*—					
Tring	368¼	Pass	5.12	Pass	5.5
Watford	382½	Pass	5.25	Pass	5.19
Willesden	394½	Pass	5.36	Pass	5.31
EUSTON	400	Arrive	5.45	Arrive	5.40

NOTE.—When owing to heavy traffic The Royal Scot in either direction is run in two sections, the Symington stop is omitted and the times shown above are subject to slight variation.

Left:
Although 'The Royal Scot' did not stop at Crewe, a booklet to commemorate the 1933 North American tour, *The Triumph of the Royal Scot*, noted passing times. *Author*

the West Coast main line image, which became somewhat tarnished because of the tremendous amount of work needed for 25kV electrification. It called at Stafford rather than Crewe.

Anglo Scottish Night Expresses

The most magical journey I knew from Crewe began when I caught the 'Royal Highlander', slipped into a sleeping berth and woke up in a summer's dawn to find the sun rising over the

Above:
'Royal Scot' in transition: an Up service approaching Crewe headed by Class 50s Nos 415 and 426 on 1 July 1970. This was a period when the Class 50s were providing improved power and speed for Anglo-Scottish expresses before electrification was completed progressively northwards from Weaver Junction to Glasgow. *A. W. Hobson*

Below:
Electrically-hauled Up 'Royal Scot' passes Stableford, south of Whitmore, headed by No 87008 *City of Liverpool* on 27 May 1978 — four years after completion of West Coast electrification. *K. Connolly*

Above:

The bulbous front ends of the LMS streamliners lacked the grace of those of their LNER rivals. Eric Treacy took what he described as 'an unusual view' of Princess Coronation No 6223 *Princess Alice* about to depart from Crewe with a West of England express it would haul as far as Shrewsbury. *Eric Treacy*

mountains north of Perth. There was glorious contrast between the heat and stickiness of Crewe's low-roofed platforms on a summer evening and the mountain air, cool and fresh, that flooded into the compartment. That was in the days before BR sleepers were air conditioned.

Sleeping car passengers could not relish the joys of Highland dawns until there had been a considerable acceleration of the night expresses. The first of three which ran in the late Victorian years departed Euston at 8.00pm and called at Crewe at 11.49pm. It did not begin pounding the Highland line north of Perth until 7.50am — long after dawn.

Bradshaw's of summer 1885 showed the 8pm as the 'Highland Express'. If a passenger had a copy of that year's *Thorough Guides to Scotland* by the respected travel writer M. J. B. Baddeley, they might have read that the West Coast was the 'oldest route to Scotland and still deservedly retains a large share of public patronage'. Baddeley dismissed the first 200 plus miles north of Euston: 'There is no scenery worth mentioning upon it until Lancaster is passed.'

A decade later there might not have been time for some passengers to see much north of Lancaster for that was the year when the 'Railway races to the North' reached their climax. Among the memorable runs was one by the little 'Jumbo' 2-4-0 No 790 *Hardwicke* which averaged 67.2mph over the 141 miles between Crewe and Carlisle. Crewe was always an important staging point for the night expresses. Apart from engine change, it was the stop where the guard of the Up service had to report if he had been asked for a stop to be made at Bletchley. Only sleeping car passengers could make such a request.

The long and heavy night sleepers made longer stops at Crewe than daytime expresses. In the 1950s, the 7.20pm Euston-Inverness sleeper

Left:
Spotters paid more attention to the Stanier Pacifics — unchallenged 'giants' of the Crewe scene — than to the two-coach motor trains. A group of spotters with feet wedged comfortably in the latticework of the footbridge watch 'Pacific' No 6254 *City of Stoke-on-Trent* taking water while working the 10.08am Euston-Perth express on 13 September 1947. *W. Philip Conolly.*

Below left:
Not all Anglo-Scottish expresses were hauled by the most powerful locomotives. On 21 August 1946, Class 5 No 5373 was in charge of a Perth-Euston express of 11 bogies. *W. Hubert Foster*

Below:
4-6-0 locomotives of two companies double head an Up express in 1935. 'Claughton' class *Sir Francis Dent*, LNWR No 2221 and LMS No 5927, pilots 'Royal Scot' No 6142, then named *Lion*. *Ian Allan Library*

reached Crewe at 10.16pm and occupied either platform No 1 or 2 for 15min. The Crewe Arrival and Departure Timetable, which staff were instructed 'must be kept strictly private and must not be given to the Public', stated that stops included Motherwell (not advertised) and also Dalnaspidal and Dalwhinnie on notice being given to the guard. Between Aviemore and Inverness calls were made at every station: Carrbridge, Tomatin, Moy, Daviot and Culloden Moor. With the exception of Carrbridge, all have closed. Like so many others on the West Coast and Highland lines, they served villages where stations, though not trains, have long passed into history.

So has part of a main line over which a Crewe-stopping sleeping car service once ran. This was the 7.30pm Euston-Perth, due Crewe platform No 3 after a run from Euston which took 30min longer than the 7.20pm. It carried a portion for Stranraer Harbour, which was detached at Carlisle and ran from Dumfries over a route closed to passengers in 1965, two years after the Beeching Report — the Portpatrick & Wigtownshire Joint via Newton Stewart.

Several named expresses which ran to the resorts and ports on the Lancashire Coast made fast, non-stop runs between Euston and Crewe. A Euston-Blackpool express service became possible after Grouping and was exploited by the LMS. The service ended, amid national and local protest, in September 1992.

For years 'The Ulster Express' ran between Euston and Fleetwood and later, Heysham Harbour.

Euston-Liverpool Express Services

For years operators estimated that up to 10min could be saved by cutting out stops at Crewe. Such a saving was made by the LNWR in 1905 when it introduced a non-stop evening dining

Below:
Two '5XP' 4-6-0s provided unusual power for the 'Red Rose' express on 2 May 1956. 'Patriot' No 45538 *Giggleswick* piloted 'Royal Scot' No 46144 *Honourable Artillery Company* because several Edge Hill (8A) shedded 'Pacifics' were in shops. *C. Williams*

car express from Liverpool to Euston. This was the company's longest non-stop route at that time. The new service was necessary to replace a Liverpool service which had joined the 5.30pm Manchester-Euston at Crewe, but the combined train had become too heavy 'even for "Precursors" ', to quote Charles Rous-Marten's 'British Locomotive Practice and Performance' column in *The Railway Magazine.*

Non-stop expresses were still to be found in the LNWR timetables early in World War 1, the October 1915 showing a 5.55pm Euston departure of the 'Liverpool Dining Car Express' due Liverpool Lime Street 9.45pm. The service also carried a second title in the same column: 'Belfast Boat Express — Via Liverpool'.

There was also a variety of other titled, or rather sub-titled expresses such as 'Breakfast Car', although this was available only between Euston (dep 8.30am) and Crewe (arr 11.47am). No such pleasure was available to passengers for the rest of the journey to Liverpool (arr 12.33pm). Departing Euston at 10.25am was a 'Luncheon Car Express' followed at 2.35pm by a rather daintily named 'Tea Car Express'.

A train that has a permanent place in railway history is the 'Merseyside Express', not least because locomotive enthusiasts will associate it always with the 'turbine locomotive', No 6202, built experimentally in an attempt to reduce coal and water consumption of big engines.

The 'Merseyside Express' was among the earliest named trains after the formation of the LMS. It never had a booked stop at Crewe, making a non-stop journey in just over 3½hr in the 1930s. Despite the introduction of more powerful locomotives, the schedule was only about 15min faster than those of the LNWR, but it was much heavier, carrying a two or three coach portion for Southport, worked forward from Liverpool Lime Street.

To celebrate the Festival of Britain in 1951, a new express 'The Red Rose' was introduced. The Down service ran non-stop in 3hr 45min. The same overall timing was given to the Up service even though it made a four minute stop at Crewe from 6.11pm, 41min after departure from Liverpool.

Pocket-size publicity leaflets given to passengers showed the Crewe passing time for the Down service as 3.28pm — two minutes under three hours from Euston.

The only named service is now 'The Merseyside Pullman', of which the Down morning service calls at Crewe and is allowed 41min to Liverpool, including a set-down stop at Runcorn (where a few passengers regularly join). The balanced late afternoon working — 16.10 from Liverpool Lime Street — runs non-stop between

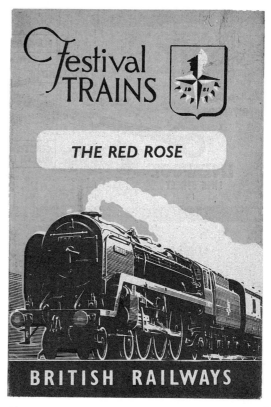

Above:
Running between Euston and Liverpool Lime Street, the 'Red Rose' was introduced to celebrate the Festival of Britain in 1951. The Down service ran non-stop, but the Up train was booked to stop for four minutes from 6.11pm in the same overall timing of 3hr 45min. *Author's collection*

Runcorn and Stafford on a journey with an overall timing of 2hr 30min. InterCity expresses to Birmingham and Poole and Liverpool-Cardiff Class 158 DMUs take just under three quarters of an hour. All stop at Runcorn and some at Hartford.

London-Liverpool Boat Expresses

Two other named restaurant car expresses between London and Liverpool could loosely be termed boat trains in the sense that they were advertised as making connections with Irish Sea ferries. 'The Shamrock', which stopped at Crewe in both directions, was timed for Liverpool-Belfast and Liverpool-Dublin sailings.

'The Manxman' was timed for Isle of Man ferry sailings to and from Douglas. The Down service took 3hr 55min including a stop at

Crewe. The Up service ran non-stop between Crewe and Rugby. At Liverpool special buses took ferry passengers to and from Lime Street station and either the Princes Landing Stage or the Irish ferry terminals in a nearby dock.

There were better arrangements for ocean liner passengers for whom special expresses were run direct to Riverside station beside Princes Landing Stage. They never appeared in public timetables and their progress through Crewe was to be found in small print in the 'dep' column of Crewe passenger working timetables. The timings reflected the pattern of the landfall and departure pattern of liners which sailed regularly all over the world, though mostly to and from America and Canada. Cunard and Canadian Pacific were the most frequently seen on carriage roof boards.

In their final years the expresses were never as grandiose as the 'Special Express Vestibuled Trains' which the LNWR stated 'perform the journey in Four Hours', using initial capital letters to emphasize speed.

The paths showed Up trains running through Crewe in mid-morning with homecoming passengers who had disembarked from liners after an early breakfast.'2 through line' was also shown as available in early afternoon for Down boat expresses with passengers whose ships were due to sail from the Mersey at the traditional hour of around 5pm.

As Crewe was the largest, most congested and slowest speed restricted junction between London and Liverpool, it was perhaps the one outward bound passengers were conscious of the most. It was also among the last British railway junctions many would see for years because in the days of Empire and before the advent of the airliner, overseas postings often lasted several years.

All the boat train paths in the Crewe timetable were suffixed by the letter 'Q' - denoting 'Runs when required'.

The last boat trains ran in winter 1971 when Riverside station closed because the liner services had ebbed away from the Mersey as a result of airline competition.

London-Manchester Services

Mancunians have always been more fortunate than Liverpudlians in their railway links with London, having all through the golden age of railways three routes by which to travel. Until a May day in 1969 they could travel a scenic route through the Peak District between Manchester Central and St Pancras.

Since then their choice has been limited to two — via Crewe or Stoke-on-Trent and the Potteries — which unite at Colwich and share the common stem of the West Coast main line for the remaining 127 miles to Euston.

While a daily Liverpool express carried a Southport portion, some Manchester services carried one for northeast Lancashire, rather further afield.

The value of two routes was exploited by the LNWR which paid the North Staffordshire Railway for running its own Manchester-Euston expresses through the Potteries. One reason was that it was quicker than via Crewe. In 1885, for example, the 12.00 noon from Euston reached Manchester London Road in 4hr 15min — 15min quicker than the 5.00pm service via Crewe. The 4.00pm departure was shown in *Bradshaw's* as 'Manchester Express', a label not given to the Crewe-routed service. Additionally, a vertical-column note made the distinction that the 4.00pm 'Runs to Manchester *via* the Potteries'.

Footnotes in the local timetables of the NSR stated that horses and private carriages were not conveyed by the Manchester-London expresses, which 'do not run in connection with other Main or Branch Line Trains'.

The practice of Manchester expresses running one way by one route and returning by the other has been common for years. Stoke has always been jealous of its London services and more run via the city than through Crewe. Besides being well-used and profitable, they also ease pressure at Crewe.

This was the case of two crack expresses of the 1930s. The Up 'Mancunian' departed at 9.45am and after running non-stop from Wilmslow reached Euston at 1.00pm. The Down departure in late afternoon at 4.10pm ran via Stoke-on-Trent and took 3hr 50min.

The 'Lancastrian', which was named by the LMS in 1927, ran to Euston via the Potteries at lunchtime and returned via Crewe in the evening on a 20min quicker schedule, often with more powerful 'Royal Scot' or 'Princess Coronation' Pacifics in charge. The Potteries route was slower because of locomotive restrictions with nothing above '5XP' allowed and so 'Jubilees' were usually diagrammed.

Right:
When Crewe platforms are almost deserted by passengers, they remain busy with rail and Post Office staff handling a brace of mail trains which arrive in quick succession to exchange traffic. Before station remodelling, the York-Shrewsbury mail made up of two TPOs and passenger coaches awaits connections. The locomotive is No 47560 *Tamar* and the date is 7 May 1982. *M. A. Norrington*

Above:
Most Manchester-Birmingham expresses run via Stoke and Stafford, rather than Crewe, to serve the Potteries. Passing Norton Bridge, now the only station between Stafford and Crewe and used only by stopping trains, is the 09.06 Birmingham New Street - Manchester Piccadilly headed by class 86/4 No 86429 'The Times'. It is about to cross the West Coast Up Fast main line to reach the former NSR branch to Stone. *C. J. Tuffs*

In its final paths before electrification, the 'Mancunian' took 3hr 40min, with Wilmslow the only stop in each direction. Flagship of the route today is 'The Manchester Pullman', which includes a sprint between Watford Junction and Wilmslow in its 2hr 29min schedule. The Down afternoon service sets down at Crewe.

From 1932 there was a third London-Manchester named express the 'Comet', which was heavily patronised up to its withdrawal in the 1960s.

Before World War 2 it ran via Crewe in both directions but afterwards when its name was transferred to another working, the Down service was routed via Stoke.

For many years the Down 'Comet' carried portions for two Merseyside destinations, detaching at Crewe, six rear coaches for Liverpool and a composite brake for Birkenhead Woodside, via Chester.

Crewe-Yorkshire

'A branch running in a north easterly direction serves Stockport, Manchester, Leeds, Bradford, York and the north east, a most extensive manufacturing district.'

Although the line primarily served Manchester, G. Shaw, editor of the *Tourists' Picturesque Guide to the London & North Western Railway*, 1876 edition, was right to draw attention to this being the company's trans-Pennine route from Crewe.

For many years it had an importance that is hard to appreciate now, especially since 1992 when the Stockport-Stalybridge service was reduced to one public passenger train a *week* running Fridays only at 13.56 from Stockport.

The LNWR showed Crewe connections in its North Eastern route timetables: LNWR from Liverpool to Leeds; North Eastern Railway (NER) beyond and stated in a footnote: 'Tickets between Leeds and London are available via Manchester in either direction'.

The North Eastern route was used by services carrying through coaches between Yorkshire and Mid Wales. Cambrian Railways timetables showed a 9.00am departure from Leeds to Aberystwyth, due 3.35pm. It called Crewe at 11.49am.

Crewe-Chester-Holyhead

Welsh aspirations that the Crewe-Chester-Holyhead route may be electrified in the future were reflected at a ceremony in March 1981 when class 86 electric locomotive No 86348 was named *Sir Clwyd — County of Clwyd*. It was the first BR locomotive to carry a bilingual name. The naming was at Crewe as the nearest point to Clwyd reached by main line electrification.

Crewe is featured in a bilingual timetable issued by Regional Railways for Manchester, Crewe, Chester, Bangor and Holyhead services. Table 83 in the BR Passenger Timetable titles 'The Irish Mail' only in English, but another Euston-Holyhead service as 'Y Draig Gymreig/The Welsh Dragon'.

Many Class 158-operated Regional Railways services along the North Wales coast start and terminate at Crewe, which no longer has the volume of through trains that once ran on the route, especially on summer Saturdays.

In late Victorian days, Crewe-Chester express timings were about 30min. Some made request stops at Beeston Castle & Tarporley. Local services which stopped at the five intermediate stations took between 40 and 47min.

Today with all these stations closed Euston-Holyhead HSTs and Class 158 DMUs take about 20min; slightly less if they make uninterrupted approaches to Crewe and Chester.

BR steam specials hauled by locomotives based temporarily at 'The Railway Age' recall memories of summer Saturdays when the route was at its most fascinating, congested with specials and relief trains to scheduled services carrying holidaymakers to the North Wales coast in their thousands.

As the nearest seaside, the North Wales resorts were always popular with the people of the Potteries, and the North Staffordshire was allowed to run its own expresses to Llandudno via Crewe.

From 1927 the Stoke line was used by workmen's trains to Crewe locomotive works. During World War 2 there was a Blythe Bridge departure at 6.21am, reaching Crewe station at 7.32am and the works halt six minutes later.

Above left:
There has never been an outstandingly fast service between North and South Wales. Most passengers prefer trains routed via Crewe than over the Shrewsbury & Chester. On 17 September 1986 Class 33 No 33005 headed the 14.08 Holyhead-Cardiff. *R. S. M. Brown*

Left:
The North Staffordshire Railway always regarded its summer trains to North Wales coast resorts as among its most prestigious. 4-4-0 No 38 leaves Rhyl with a Wakes holiday special from Stoke to Llandudno in July 1919. *Hugh Oliver collection*

Shrewsbury & Crewe

Among expresses introduced by the GWR after the Severn Tunnel opened was a Bristol-Crewe, experimentally run in summer 1888. It was an almost immediate success and eight years later the GWR announced a new morning express from Bristol and Cardiff to Scotland, and an improved express service between the West of England, the Northwest and Yorkshire and Scotland. Crewe was listed among stations where passengers could break their journey.

For many years the route was busy with night expresses including a 2am departure from Crewe of an express carrying sleeping cars from Manchester to Plymouth and through coaches to Penzance.

It was followed less than half an hour later by the York to Swansea mail, which also carried passengers.

The route retained its shape until 1970 when long distance expresses were switched via Birmingham. Since then the Shrewsbury and Crewe has been served by Manchester/Liverpool-Cardiff trains, presently '158 trains', to quote BR leaflets which, in October 1991, announced an overall speed-up, with Manchester and Shrewsbury linked in 1hr 20min. This is 45min faster than in LNWR days when Crewe-Shrewsbury non-stop timings were 45min.

Today, timings are 30min for Class 158s, 45min for trains stopping at six intermediate stations, of which Prees and Yorton are request stops. Four stopping trains are extended over the Central Wales line to Swansea to form Crewe's longest stopping train service, only two miles shorter than the 158 miles to Euston.

Long distance services were also found in LNWR timetables covering Cambrian Railways trains to the Mid Wales coast over its main line from Whitchurch.

Above:

Cheap and handy pocket timetables were popular for years. Those published by Phillipson & Golder of Chester detailed bus and train services over a wide area, including Crewe and Stafford local trains. This example dates from January 1951. *Author's collection*

Advertised connection times at Whitchurch in 1915 varied up to 49min. When Whitchurch-Welshpool closed 50 years later, they still could!

The Great Western presence at Crewe had started on 20 October 1863 when the Nantwich & Market Drayton Railway was opened to passenger services. At first separated from the rest of the GWR system, there was a service of four trains each way between Crewe and Market

Right:
Occasionally, smart and powerful NSR tanks handled the excursions. NSR 'K' class 4-4-2 No 14 heads a train of LNWR six-wheel coaches off the Chester line past North box.
Bucknall collection

Right:
Double-headed power for a Swansea-Manchester express, in the summer of 1955. 'Jubilee' class 4-6-0 No 45735 *Comet* pilots Class 5 No 45311 out of the old platform No 3 at Crewe. A Class 4 0-6-0 stands in an adjacent platform where modernisation work has begun. The run-down state of the station at that time is evident from crumbling platform edges and grass growing between slabs. *Brian Morrison*

Below right:
Before the introduction of two-car Class 158s, Manchester/Liverpool-Cardiff services were made up of a variety of locomotive-hauled trains. Class 33 No 33017 passes the village station at Wrenbury with the 16.01 Crewe-Cardiff of six coaches on 10 July 1981. *Peter Kynaston*

Below:
Deputising for a failed 'Sprinter' unit, Class 37 No 37407 *Loch Long* departs north with a Cardiff-Liverpool service on 14 February 1989. *M. T. Holley*

Above:
The Cambrian Railways regularly worked trains into Crewe from Whitchurch, terminus of its main line to Cardigan Bay. It also loaned three locomotives to the LNWR during World War 1. About 1918, 0-6-0 No 93 leaves Crewe for the north with LNWR corridor stock. *W. H. Whitworth*

Drayton on weekdays with a fifth on Wednesdays. The southern section, from Market Drayton to Wellington, opened on 16 October 1867 and services were extended southwards. Although the line was largely operated by local services, the completion of the route allowed for the introduction of a number of through services — such as that to Manchester (London Road) in

Below:
Cambrian locomotives were serviced at North Shed and a tender piled high with coal suggests 0-6-0 No 92 had been on shed before working a passenger service. *W. H. Whitworth*

1867 and one from Worcester to Crewe — although these were gradually withdrawn. That the line was increasingly regarded as a rural backwater so far as passenger services were concerned is emphasized by the fact that the section was the last part of the GWR network to be operated by 'time interval', a practice which continued until August 1891.

By summer 1932 the service comprised seven Down and six Up services on weekdays with two each way on Sundays. By 1947 this was reduced to five each way on weekdays, although there remained two services each way on Sundays.

The 1963 withdrawal of passenger trains between Crewe and Wellington had reduced the number of trains stopping at Nantwich. GWR local services stopped there through the years, but did not call at the two LNWR motor halts.

Nantwich was the first of eight stations and five halts in the 32 miles and trains were

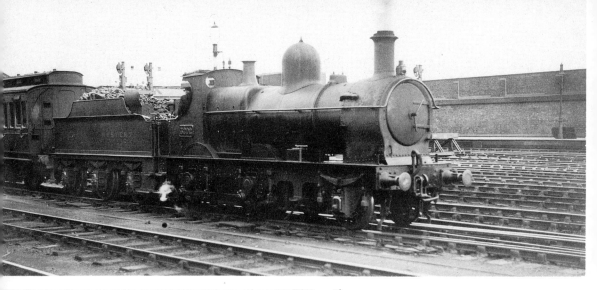

Above:
Vintage locomotives often worked GWR local services in North Shropshire. 'Stella' class 2-4-0 No 3202 leaves Crewe with a stopping train to Wellington about 1920. *R. W. Miller collection*

allowed about 1hr 15min. In the last years of the line there were seven weekday trains starting with the 6.5am booked from No 3 Bay at Crewe. After Nationalisation the last Down train was speeded up by 5min, being scheduled into No 2 Bay at Crewe at 10.42pm. The Sunday service was of two semi-fast trains which stopped only at Nantwich, Market Drayton and Tern Hill, a station much used by service personnel.

Stoke-on-Trent-Derby and Nottingham

The Crewe-Stoke-East Midlands line carries some 17 trains a day in each direction. All but four begin and end journeys at Nottingham or further east, including a Skegness service.

All trains between Crewe and Stoke stop at Alsager and Kidsgrove and some additionally at

Above left:
Clerestory coaches were often found on Crewe-Wellington trains. GWR 'Bird' class 4-4-0 No 3445 *Flamingo* leaves Crewe in 1936. Large water tank on platform end. *R. W. Miller collection*

Left:
Closure in 1965 of the Oswestry, Ellesmere and Whitchurch section of the former Cambrian main line robbed Crewe of a source of local trains. On 18 June 1962, the 12.15pm Welshpool-Manchester service, headed by 4-6-0 No 7802 *Bradley Manor* (later preserved), runs into a rather deserted platform at Ellesmere. *Ian Allan Library*

Longport and Etruria. Times taken by DMUs vary between 18min for those not calling at Longport and Etruria, and 25min for all-station services. In steam days best timings were between 38min and 44min, with calls at two long-closed stations, Chatterley and Radway Green & Barthomley. At 4¾ miles this was the station nearest Crewe.

A summer Saturday service from Nottingham to Llandudno is a descendant of an NSR service which the Company ran exercising running powers negotiated with the LNWR.

Cross Country Services

The biggest changes have been in the pattern of cross country express services between Scotland, Northwest England and southern England from Penzance to Dover.

All run via Crewe and Birmingham, inheritors of Northwest-West of England services which ran via Shrewsbury and the Severn Tunnel.

'The Pines Express' between Liverpool/Manchester and Bournemouth became so well established through the years that the name survives in current BR timetables, although it has long deserted Crewe. For many years the southbound service stopped in platform No 5 from 11.02am-11.20am before leaving for its next public-timetabled stop at Cheltenham Spa, although in fact it made an unadvertised one at Birmingham New Street.

It reached Bournemouth over the Somerset & Dorset from Bath. Since the closure of that route it has run via Reading. Today it links Manchester and Poole through the Potteries and no longer carries a Liverpool portion, which before World War 2 was often confined to a single

UP TRAINS—Weekdays—continued.

Train.	FROM	TO	Re-port-ing No.	CREWE. Arr.	CREWE. Dep.	Platform No.	REMARKS.
a.m. 10 20	Manchester ...	Bournemouth	220	a.m. 11 2	a.m. 11 20	5	(1) Bournemouth, (2) Birmingham, forward 11.12. Stops at Birmingham (not advertised), Cheltenham Spa, Gloucester Eastgate, Bath Green Park, Evercreech Jn., Blandford, Broadstone and Poole.
9 35	Liverpool (Riverside)	Euston	472	...	11 4	5	(FO). "Q." Crewe North Jn. arr. 10*47, dep. 11*2.
9 10	Llandudno ...	Euston	56	11 6	11 27	3	Stops at Stafford, Lichfield (SO) (to pick up only), Tamworth (SO) (to pick up only), Nuneaton, Rugby Midland, Northampton, Wolverton, Bletchley, Leighton Buzzard, Watford Jn. (SX). Attaches dining vehicles rear.
11 20	Crewe	Derby Midland	...	...	11 20	6 Bay ...	Stops at Alsager, Kidsgrove Cen., Longport, Etruria, Stoke, Longton, Meir, Blythe Bridge and stations to Derby Midland (except Egginton and Pear Tree & N.).
11 58	Port Sunlight	Alsager Jn. ...	...	11*22	11*40	6 Platform Line	(SX). Class F. Empties.
6 5	Carlisle	Crewe	274	11 38	...	5	———
10 43	Runcorn ...... (Folly Lane)	Alsager Jn. ...	...	11W49	11W56	6 Platform line	Class : F. Empties.
6 35	Workington ...	Euston	70	p.m. 12 1	p.m. 12 9	5	(SO). Is regular, not advertised, until 3rd October, 1953 inclusive. "Q" commencing 10th October, 1953. Stops at Stafford.
10 55	Birkenhead ...	Crewe	178	12‡ 2	...	3	(SX). (‡—P.B. 12.6). Conveys London vehicles forward 12.20 p.m.
p.m. 12 10	Crewe	Shrewsbury ...	...	...	12 10	4 Bay ...	Stops at all stations.
a.m. 10 0	Blackpool (Cen.)	Euston	330	12‡10	12 18	4	(SO). (‡—P.B. 12.11). Stops at Stafford.
10 0	Blackpool (C.)	Euston	330	12‡10	12‡20	4	(SX). Stops at Stafford. (‡—P.B. arr. 12.11, dep. 12.18). Attaches vehicles off 10.55 a.m. Birkenhead to Crewe.
8 25	Holyhead......	Crewe	72	12 18	...	3	(SO).
p.m. 12 20	Crewe	Derby Midland	...	...	12‡20	5 Bay ...	(SO). (‡—P.B. 12.18). Stops at all stations to Blythe Bridge then Leigh, Uttoxeter, Sudbury, Tutbury, Pear Tree & N.
a.m. 11 10	Manchester ...	Crewe	...	12 20	...	6	———
p.m. 12†26	Crewe Brook Sdgs.	Wolverton Works	232	...	12†26	Brook Sidings	(MSX). "Q."

Crewe arr. & dep.—C

coach. It was marshalled into a Liverpool-Birmingham express scheduled to reach Crewe one minute ahead of the main express. Birmingham was reached in 2hr 22min from Liverpool — among the fastest timings on that route in the 1930s.

Changing Patterns of Local Passenger Services

Half of the six routes radiating from Crewe have lost their local passenger services: those to Chester, Stafford and Warrington. The Shrewsbury line is the only one to have lost its role as a route of long distance expresses as the North Staffordshire Derby line via Stoke-on-Trent never carried any. The only 'branch line' service

for which Crewe was a terminal was that between Sandbach and Northwich.

The biggest loss on the Crewe scene brought about by modernisation, and especially the end of steam, has been in locomotive variety. Stopping trains had an especial appeal for spotters because the types of locomotives were unpredictable, especially during the war years.

There were no locomotive weight or clearance restrictions on the main lines and so any available engine could be used to maintain stopping services often heavily used by workers to get to and from their homes when bus routes were curtailed because of petrol rationing. When a signal was pulled off and a lineside spotter knew a local train was due there was always the pleasure of anticipating something unusual. The sight of a streamlined 'Coronation' at the head of a slow train of three old compartment coaches was incongruous. But what a delight: a memory recalled half a century later with the ease of one of only yesterday!

Grand Junction North of Crewe: Liverpool and Warrington Local Services

The setting of 1943 was on the Down slow line at Speke as a summer's evening stopper from Crewe was preparing to call at West Allerton. A now unsolvable mystery remains as to whether the locomotive was running in after being overhauled in the Works (the paint work was bright, rather than shining), or it was working the stopping link as the best available locomotive.

The Crewe-Liverpool service had a splendid variety of motive power. In the late 1930s and through the years of World War 2 local trains were often headed by veteran LNWR locomo-

tives: 'Claughton', 'Prince of Wales' and 19in goods 4-6-0s and 'Precursor' and 'George V' class 4-4-0s. Only gradually were they replaced by 'Black Five' 4-6-0s and Fowler and Stanier 2-6-2Ts and 2-6-4Ts.

Today, if the EMUs stop at all nine intermediate stations between Crewe and Liverpool — and few do — they take 52min for the 35½ miles.

The Crewe-Liverpool diagram has always been the backbone of stopping services over the West Coast route north of Crewe, but until Preston Brook closed just after Nationalisation, there were occasional trains stopping all stations between Crewe and Warrington. This service was supplemented by a few one-class only trains between Acton Bridge and Warrington. While both stations remain open, there is no service between them.

The service was neither frequent nor fast. In May 1860 the LNWR was running four Down and three Up trains, and allowed 45min for the 24 miles if they called at all six intermediate stations. Some missed Minshull Vernon.

The service changed little through the years and after World War 2 when the number of intermediate stations had been reduced to four, local trains were still allowed 43min. InterCity electrics link the towns in 18min non-stop, although a few call at Hartford.

Crewe-Manchester Local Services

The variety of trains — and motive power — on the Manchester route is sometimes seen in early evening when three services depart from Crewe within a few minutes.

If the Cardiff-Manchester is a few minutes late, it waits in platform No 5 for the departure of the Down 'Manchester Pullman' from platform No 6 at 17.54 while in platform No 1 the 17.43 all-stations waits for both to leave.

The 'Pullman' is booked to take 44min to Piccadilly; the Cardiff — usually a Class 158 DMU — is allowed 49min and the stopper 57min.

The Cardiff trains provide the most frequent of semi-fast services, augmented by InterCity services to Birmingham International (though most run via Stoke), Poole and Brighton.

When a Class 304 EMU left Crewe at 18.27 on Christmas Eve 1991, some passengers did not know that it was the last through train to Altrincham before the service was cut back to Deansgate, with trains reversing in a shunting neck forming what is now the tip of the Manchester South Junction & Altrincham (MSJ & A). The rest of the route to Altrincham has been converted to Metrolink.

The change was the biggest to local services since the conversion of the MSJ & A from 1,500V dc to 25kV in May 1971. It robbed the Crewe service of local trains which occasionally became expresses in mid journey. It happened when trains were late reaching Manchester Piccadilly. In order to make up time, they ran non-stop from Oxford Road to Altrincham after passengers for intermediate stations were asked to transfer to a following train.

All Crewe-Deansgate trains run via Stockport following the switching to the main line of several which used the Styal Loop.

A 1992 innovation was the introduction of a semi-fast locomotive-hauled service at 07.56 from Crewe, calling only at Sandbach, Alderley Edge, Wilmslow and Stockport.

The slam-door Class 304 EMUs, in service since 1960, have been replaced by Class 305s from the Liverpool Street and Fenchurch Street routes. They have a 53min booking between Crewe and Manchester Piccadilly, calling at 11 stations, and are allowed a further 7min between Piccadilly and Deansgate.

The timings have changed little since electrification in 1960, the service never having lived up to the high hopes at that time for the development of South Manchester suburban services. But they are much quicker than in steam days when LMS timings were about 1hr 20min. They were virtually the same as they had been in LNWR days when that company planned to increase traffic and built the Styal line and Mayfield station to relieve congestion at London Road station.

The 'Manchesters' have always been the most intensive of Crewe's local services, although in 1992 they were drastically reduced on Sundays, the first Up stopping service being the 17.33 from Piccadilly.

Push-and-Pull or Motor Trains

Crewe push-and-pull trains added variety to local services. Trains were allowed the same 8min timings between Crewe and Sandbach as other local services.

Northwich was reached in 33min from Crewe after a stop at Middlewich, the only station on the Sandbach-Northwich branch after the 1942 closure of LNWR motor halts at Cledford Bridge and Billinge Green. These two stations were used by only half of the eight weekday only services.

For years the push-and-pull trains were a familiar sight in Nos 9 and 10 North bays at Crewe. Their spirit was captured in a commemorative brochure for farewell tours of northwest push-and-pull routes run by the Locomotive Club of Great Britain in February 1966. It reflected: 'There is probably nothing more synonymous with the dying age of the railways than Push-and-Pull trains. On former LMS lines they have largely gone unsung. Perhaps this is because they operated over lines which saw other, more grandiose services where the little 2-6-2 tank in the back platform or bay was often overshadowed by the "Scot" or "Jubilee" on the through line.'

After the Northwich local service was withdrawn from 4 January 1960, the branch remained open for freight routed via Crewe and passenger diversions. Before Grouping about half of the motor trains were extended beyond Northwich to and from the West Coast main line at Acton Bridge. They were cut back to Northwich from 30 June 1941. Further economies were made and only four daily Crewe-Northwich trains were running when the service was withdrawn. For years the LNWR served Knutsford with two Down and one Up train between Manchester (Oxford Road), Northwich and Crewe, where Euston connections were advertised. The LMS abandoned the service in 1933.

Passenger Trains over Independent Lines

The Independent Lines have strong appeal to railtour organisers and the passengers they attract, especially as so few passenger trains now use them. Years ago they were busy as diversionary routes at holiday times, especially in summer, and on August Bank Holiday 1938 the LMS diverted more than 70 services running to and from Liverpool, Manchester and Chester and North Wales over them to ease congestion through Crewe station.

Absolute block replaced permissive block working when passenger trains were running over the Lines, either at holiday times or during emergencies. The regulation changes applied to a host of the Independent Lines: Up slow between Coppenhall Junction and Coal Yard boxes; the Up and Down Liverpool, Manchester and Chester Independents; the Up and Down Salop; Up and Down fast Independent; Up and Down slow Independents.

Mail Trains

In a 405-page book, *Railway Reform: Its Importance and Practicability*, published in 1865, William Galt noted that 'the completion of the Grand Junction Railway furnished the first of those great triumphs of postal communication for which we are indebted to the railways.

'The Liverpool merchant, and still more the private individual of humbler station or less busy habits, were astounded to find letters sent from London at eight in the evening in their hands the following morning.'

Some of that mail will have travelled, via Crewe, on the first travelling post office, adapted from a horse-box which the GJR introduced between Birmingham and Liverpool on 6 January 1838. Later the same year the GJR introduced the first purpose built mail-sorting carriage. It had the first apparatus for picking up and dropping mail bags at speed.

Mail traffic through Crewe was further boosted in 1838 when a London-Bletchley TPO service was extended to Preston. When the Chester & Crewe opened in October 1840, auxiliary 'mails' were introduced between Euston and Chester, mail being taken forward to Holyhead by coach. The 'mails' were classed as auxiliary because Liverpool was the Admiralty and private mail boat port.

Because of penalties for the late running of mail trains to times and schedules laid down by the GPO, they were given priority. They were duplicated in 1843 and in 1848 'The Irish Mail' began running between Euston and Bangor, being extended through to Holyhead in 1850. It is now the oldest named train in the world and it is one that has always stopped at Crewe.

The mail that it carried was part of the volume which in 1874 earned the LNWR revenue from the Post Office of £136,740 — more than double that paid to any of some 40 railway companies then carrying mail. The second biggest carrier was the Great Western, which had a revenue of £52,500.

Among a number of main line postal services in Victorian days were the 'North Mail,' which formed the rear portion of 'The Irish Mail,' being detached at Crewe and continuing to Glasgow and Edinburgh; the 'Limited Mail,'which carried Anglo-Scottish sleepers; and the 'Auxiliary Scotch Mail.'

From them were born the trains which came to form the backbone of the services, the 'West Coast Postal Express' between Euston and sev-

Below:
The night postal scene: Class 31 No 31242 after arrival with the 20.00 Postal from Peterborough. The return working was the 00.44 to Peterborough North. The date is 31 January 1975. *David Clough*

eral Scottish destinations. The Up and Down 'Postals' or 'TPO Specials,' as they were also known, were allowed some 16min at Crewe because of the volume of mail handled.

The TPOs were withdrawn during both World Wars and when they were restored after World War 2 they ran only at nights; changes in the postal system meant that daytime services were no longer needed.

In the 1950s the 'West Coast Postal' connected at Crewe with those to and from Swansea, Stoke-on-Trent, Birmingham and Holyhead. The Down 'Postal' departed Crewe at midnight, followed five minutes later by the Swansea-York, which carried passengers and was shown in Public Timetables as departing 12.1am for Stockport Edgeley ('for postal purposes only', stated staff timetables), Huddersfield and Leeds City. Huddersfield luggage was to be loaded in the 'Swansea to York van, front end. Leeds in rear brake'.

Crewe's large postal sorting office beside the east side of the station is platform connected by subways. In 1960 Crewe officials believed that more parcel post was transferred at Crewe than at any other station. Between 200 and 300 bags of mail were regularly off-loaded from several London trains.

In the late 1960s three million letters and 200,000 parcels were being handled weekly, mostly arriving and departing by rail, additional to mail transferred direct from one train to another. Completion of main line electrification in 1967 caused problems in mail and parcels handling because stopping times were reduced.

Parcels Traffic

Inadequate parcels handling facilities plagued Crewe for years. In 1960 traffic was so heavy that a parcels sorting depot, possibly built away from the station precincts, was the only solution.

The traffic was heaviest on the Downside with practically all parcels sorted and reloaded forward at the south end of the then platform Nos 1 and 1B and 2B Bays.

About half the Downside traffic originated from the Western Region which, stated an internal report, 'invariably arrives in a very rough state and without the advantage of destination numbers marked on packages'.

At modernisation in 1985 about 30 daily parcel trains carried mail for unloading and sorting at Crewe. This was additional to mail carried on passenger trains.

Among other traffic handled at the station was fish. Consignments from Hull, Grimsby, Aberdeen and Fleetwood in the 1960s were still

Above:
Parcels traffic handled at Crewe has declined in recent years from a peak which became so heavy that the Horse Landing platform on the most westerly of the station lines was roofed-over to handle extra seasonal traffic. In 1984, No 25051 pauses in a main platform with a northbound parcels. *C. L. Shaw*

heavy enough for a foreman and two porters to be assigned to the traffic every night. There were also small consignments from other areas including South Wales.

Crewe never had newspaper trains in the sense that it had mail trains. For years large quantities of daily papers were transferred from three late evening Euston trains. Most of the papers were destined for South and Central Wales. Newspapers for the Crewe area arrived on an early morning train from Manchester which ran forward to Stoke.

For many years station staff handled 'special vans' of bulk consignments of fruit and flowers from Weymouth, Southampton and Penzance. The produce was forwarded to a number of destinations usually by passenger train.

Post Office and train load parcels traffic was reorganised into Rail express systems in 1991, the official launch taking place at Crewe Traction Maintenance Depot on 11 October. The system, with its 24hr national control in Rail House, Crewe, has its own management, and distinctively liveried locomotives and rolling stock.

Motorail Terminal

Fresh long distance passenger traffic developed from Crewe in summer 1973 when Motorail services to Scotland and Devon and Cornwall were inaugurated from a new terminal off Nantwich Road, Crewe — 'Tommy's Lane' as it was named in memory of stationmaster Humphries. They replaced services which had run from Newton-le-Willows and Sutton Coldfield. The Crewe-based services ended when Motorail services were concentrated on London Kensington.

8 Goods Services

Express and other passenger trains and their highly polished locomotives may have given Crewe its glamour, but goods gave it far more traffic. This was reflected by receipts for the LNWR as a whole. In 1908, when Basford Hall yard had been enlarged, they totalled more than £9 million for goods, mineral and livestock traffic, compared with £6.5 million for passengers, parcels and mail. The gap between goods and passenger revenues had narrowed by Grouping.

The tremendous volume of goods traffic Crewe was handling in 1938 of some 47,000 wagons a week (mentioned in Chapter 5), was probably exceeded during World War 2. A signalman at Wrinehill Box — still open — recalls an occasion when he returned to duty after a 12-hour break to find goods trains bound for Crewe were only two blocks ahead of those he had passed them through on his last shift. It was not an uncommon occurrence. The wartime traffic was handled under tremendous difficulties, not least the problems of keeping locomotives steaming while waiting for hours at signals.

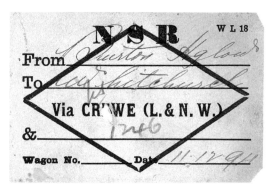

Above:
A label from a wagon that passed through Crewe in Victorian days. Dated '11.12.94', it was for a consignment from the NSR at Burton, Horninglow, to Whitchurch. *Author's collection*

Below:
One of the few notable engineering features of railways associated with Crewe is the Grand Junction's Vale Royal viaduct near Hartford. It is being crossed by an Up freight hauled by 2-10-0 No 92008 on 21 April 1954. *D. J. Beaver*

'Patriot' class 4-6-0s often worked slow freights as
they got towards the end of their working lives.
No 45505 *The Royal Army Ordnance Corps* heads an
Up freight near Hartford. It has an unusual, high-
sided tender. The date was 24 June 1961. The
overhead wires between Crewe and Liverpool were
energised on 30 September 1961 and the electric
service began on 1 January 1962. *J.Whiteley*

Traffic gradually declined after the War and a
count in summer 1960 produced a total of
34,624 wagons a week. That compared with
37,826 handled in a comparable week in 1953.
How accurate were such figures?

A BR operating report of 1960 stated that
approximately 6,000 wagons a day were then
being handled, but it pointed out that every
wagon was counted when entering one of the
subsidiary yards. A wagon arriving at Sorting
Sidings South Middle and later trip-worked to
Gresty Lane Down sidings would be counted at
both points.

The Report showed that all traffic off the
Western Region was handled at Gresty Lane
Down Sidings and trains were made up there for
Manchester, Yorkshire, Liverpool, the North and
Scotland. Trains bound for the Western Region
were made up at Gresty Green, together with
several daily Up trains conveying traffic primarily for the WR. Gresty Lane Up sidings were
then an overflow for Gresty Green. They also
sorted warehouse and wagon repair shop traffic.
Warehouse traffic was worked forward in trip
workings from Gresty Lane Down sidings to

Sorting Sidings North. Northbound trains
detached locomotives which needed servicing at
South shed. Trains from the south arriving off
the Down line and terminating in the Yard went
to Sorting Sidings Middle. Through traffic to
and from the North, Manchester, Liverpool and
Chester was dealt with in the Middle Up and
Down sidings.

In Sorting Sidings South, trips from North
Staffordshire sidings were received and primary
shunting was carried out for five groups in Middle Yard. Among long distance trains that used
them were those with wagons sent to a Group G
siding designated for traffic for the Caledonian,
Highland and LNER Great North of Scotland
areas. The wagon allocations of the Group sid-

Above:
An unusual combination of motive power: a Birmingham-Basford Hall freight with Class 9F 2-10-0 No 92009 piloting '5MT' 2-6-0 No 42950 heading north from Stafford having just passed the junctions of the Uttoxeter and Wellington branches. *J. B. Bucknall*

Above right:
A Class E goods for Basford Hall at Stafford, hauled by a Warrington (8B) shedded Class G2A 0-8-0 No 49119. Stafford station (background) was completely rebuilt during electrification, which was extended from Crewe to Stafford on 7 January 1963. *Brian Morrison*

ings was modified nightly 'in connection with the working of the Down important freight trains'. Trains from Chester bound for Stoke and Derby went to North Staffordshire Up sidings to pick up traffic from Crewe warehouse. North Staffordshire Down sidings handled similiar traffic bound for Chester and North Wales.

In this era, just over 100 trains began workings from the Yard. A similiar number terminated there and another 70 passed through. Sixteen shunting engines worked round the clock including four on intensive tripping between the yards.

At Crewe, special instructions related to the handling of locomotive coal. Staff at every traffic yard where coal was held for the sheds had to telephone the District Operating Manager's Control Room twice a day - at 6am and 4pm - to advise of stocks. Such was the volume that at times coal was stored at Nantwich Yard. It included coal from several North Staffordshire pits which was handled through North Staffordshire sidings.

There were also trains carrying large quantities of coal and coke for shipment from several ports and it was laid down that it was not to be worked forward until released by Control. In the 1950s general coal traffic was regarded as small in relation to that of the Yard. Control had also to be advised about special freight rated traffics — livestock, meat and fruit among them — which were passing, or about to pass, Crewe 'so that suitable services can be arranged'. For many years cattle traffic was heavy and animals often

needed food and water on arrival. It was provided at the Goods Warehouse sidings.

Horse traffic also passed through Crewe on long distance passenger services. Several Anglo-Scottish expresses conveyed horses and carriages to and from London.

One of the shortest workings over the West Coast main line was a daily train between the locomotive works and Basford Sand Siding (actually two) on the Up side just south of Basford Hall Junction. The trains had to shunt on and off the Up main line, controlled by Basford Sand Siding Box until its closure in 1956.

For many years one of the first departures on Monday mornings from the station was the

Right:
Mineral traffic through Crewe station: Class 47/3 No 47340 heads a loaded merry-go-round train on 27 August 1975. *Norman E. Preedy*

00.07 'Merchandise' working to Sorting Sidings North. Two minutes of its 16min journey was taken up with locomotive run round at Gresty Lane No 1.

Crewe lies at the heart of one of Britain's richest dairy farming areas and for years millions of gallons of milk were dispatched from a large dairy at Calveley on the Chester line. Yard staff had to notify Crewe control of the arrival and departure of twice daily trains and light engines 'in connection therewith'. Loaded trains routed south were booked through Crewe 13 miles after departure. A 'unique' emergency working from Calveley took place on Coronation

Day 1953 to meet an unprecedented demand for milk in London, where supplies were quickly running out.

Consideration was given to adding another freight diversionary route to the host available through Crewe after the closure of the former NSR Sandbach-Kidsgrove from 1 January 1971. With the Sandbach-Northwich branch it formed a through route between the northwest and the Potteries. The suggested diversion was through platform No 6 (now No 1), the most easterly of the Crewe platforms. It was rejected as being too costly.

GWR Goods Services via Wellington

Completion of Euston-Northwest electrification on 6 March 1967 ended the usefulness of the former GWR Wellington-Nantwich secondary line as a diversionary route between Crewe and the Midlands. It was hastily disposed of, being closed completely on 1 May 1967, almost four years after the withdrawal of local passenger services.

It was a post-Beeching economy that robbed the Crewe railway scene of one of its colourful elements for the GWR presence was stronger than was often realised. There were up to eight daily freights from Oxley Sidings, Wolverhampton, and a number of places further south.

Above:
Trains between Ford plants at Halewood, Liverpool, and Dagenham, Essex, have long been a familiar sight at Crewe. Locomotive No 86007 is seen at Gresty Lane with such a train on 2 December 1985. *J. Winkle*

Western Region Service Time Tables (sic) for summer 1955 showed through workings to Crewe from several places in the Midlands and Southern England. They included Stourbridge Junction, Kingswinford Junction, Worcester, Basingstoke and Exeter. Services from Oldbury & Langley Green ran via Crewe to Latchford and Haverton Hill, Middlesbrough.

After Grouping, most freight trains arriving at Crewe via Wellington ran direct to Basford Hall yard reception sidings, locomotives and brake vans using the yard turntable, although some detached traffic at the former LNWR sidings at Gresty Lane. But by the mid-1930s operating patterns had changed and the GWR ran mostly to its five sidings at Gresty Lane which could hold 206 wagons.

For many years both companies competed for traffic from large horse sales at Crewe. A GWR internal report stated that:

'by energetic canvassing we obtain a very good share of the traffic for London and the South.

The traffic is booked at the GWR office on the sale ground and the horses are loaded by the LMS company's staff at their stage.'

9 Locomotive Works

'The locomotive works, covering 137 acres, 48 of which are covered in, and employing about 8,000 men, form the largest and most celebrated railway establishment in the world.'

That was the LNWR's claim in the *Railway Year Book* of 1914 at the peak of the golden age of steam for which, since 1843 the works had built over 5,000 locomotives and repaired thousands more. By the time the works celebrated their 150th anniversary in 1990, the total built had risen beyond 8,000 including electric and diesel locomotives and High Speed Train power cars.

It was in 1840 that Joseph Locke, as engineer-in-chief of the Grand Junction Railway, began arranging the transfer of the company's works from Edge Hill, Liverpool, a task which was completed on 10 March 1843. Nine months later a locomotive erection and repair shop was in full use, although initially work was concentrated on repair work to existing locomotives. The first locomotive, an 'Early Crewe' type 2-2-2 called *Tamerlane*, was turned out on 20 October of the same year.

This first locomotive was never as famous as another 2-2-2 built while the works was still

Above:
The forbidding Victorian factory atmosphere lingered for years among the works buildings. The Signal Shop seen from the yard of North Shed, with the Chester line immediately behind 'Pacific' No 46237 *City of Bristol*. Far right is the works clock-tower, which housed a time-signal bell. *J. R. Carter*

Left:
An historic posed photograph inside the works with 4-4-0 No 2155 *W. C. Brocklehurst*, one of the 10 original 'George the Fifths', alongside a replica of Stephenson's *Rocket*. *Ian Allan Library*

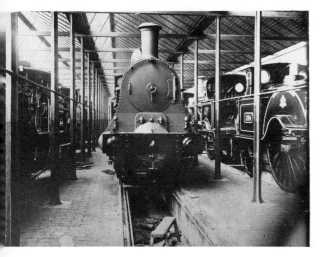

owned by the GJR: No 49 *Columbine*. It was turned out on 20 February 1845 and was the first new locomotive constructed at the works. Ninety years after it was withdrawn in 1902 it still delights the eyes of visitors to the National Railway Museum, the oldest Crewe-built locomotive to survive.

As production boomed at Crewe, work became concentrated on locomotive building and repair. This was particularly the case after 1846, when the GJR merged with the Manchester & Birmingham and London & Birmingham railways to form the London & North Western. Carriage and wagon building and repair work, which had also been expanding since the move from Edge Hill, was gradually moved away. Carriage work was concentrated at Wolverton, after being carried out for a short time at Saltley, Birmingham. The wagon workshops moved to Earlestown on the Liverpool & Manchester line near Warrington.

As Crewe Works grew so did the number of workers and the population of the town. One major development, for example, was the opening of an iron rail mill on 10 June 1853, the year in which the wagon department moved.

In 1862 the company amalgamated the Northern and Southern divisions of the railway. The Southern Division had historically been provided with locomotives built either at Wolverton Works or by outside suppliers, whilst Crewe had furnished the Northern Division with locomotives. As a result of the reorganisation,

Above:

The cramped Paint Shop always had a special appeal for visitors because, for years, it was also used as a store for preserved locomotives. But that was not always the case. The late Victorian scene of the Webb era with tender-less locomotives packed boiler to footplate: at least eight are visible. A Webb three-cyclinder compound 0-8-0 stands alongside single, No 184 *Problem*. *Ian Allan Library*

Below:

The works boiler shop shown in the 1876 edition of the *Tourists' Picturesque Guide*. It stated that: 'out of 2,500 locomotive boilers made at Crewe since 1855, and up to the end of June 1875, there has not been a single case of explosion.' *Author's collection*

John Ramsbottom, based at Crewe, became the locomotive superintendent and mechanical engineer for the whole system.

1862 was also the year of the inauguration of Ramsbottom's 18in gauge works tramway, which was eventually to stretch for some five miles through the works and connect with the station. After dismantling in LMS days, *Pet*, one of the system's seven small engines, was preserved. It was built at Crewe, to a design by Ramsbottom, in 1865 and was withdrawn in 1929.

By 1864 the last of the land vacant at the 'old works' site had been used and a Bessemer steel plant had to be built a short distance down the Chester & Holyhead line. This led to the deviation of the line a little to the south, and the 'Deviation Shops' were built in the fork between the lines and occupied by millwrights, pattern-makers and moulders in 1867.

This was a year ahead of the opening of the deviation and a year after the 1,000th locomotive had been built: a Ramsbottom 'DX' class six-coupled express goods engine with open footplate.

The 2,000th engine, a small 2-4-0 passenger tank came off the works in July 1876. The last

survivor of the class, later BR No 58092, worked on the Cromford & High Peak Railway until the early 1950s.

The 3,000th locomotive, a Webb three-cylinder compound 2-2-2-2 passenger tank received extra attention for its completion was celebrated as part of the 1887 Jubilee Rejoicings. They fell almost half way through the reign between 1871 and 1903 of Francis W. Webb as Locomotive Superintendent of the company. He remains the best known of the Victorians who dominated the Crewe scene. When he retired, the LNWR chairman, Lord Stalbridge, said that almost from its very beginning he had been the mainspring of the greatest of their manufacturing departments.

In his book *North Western. A Saga of the Premier Line of Great Britain 1846-1922*, O. S. Nock asserts that the work of Webb will be discussed as long as there are railways. Ninety-one of his famous 'Cauliflower' 0-6-0 goods engines, which he designed in the Jubilee Year, were still in some of the earliest of my Ian Allan *ABC of LMS Locomotives* bought in the 1940s. So were his coal traffic 0-6-0s which he built two years after taking office.

Webb was also designer of the 4,000th locomotive, a 'Jubilee' 4-4-0 compound *La France*, which soon after completion in March 1900 went on exhibition in Paris.

By then there had been major developments of the works so that locomotive construction was concentrated in new workshops and repairs in the old works.

Right:
A fascinating variety of elderly locomotives shunted the works. LNWR 0-4-2ST No 3248 is seen in action with wagons of three companies: North Staffordshire, LNWR and Great Central. *Jim Peden collection*

Below right:
Two of Webb's 0-4-2 with square saddle tanks dating from 1896-1901, were eventually taken into BR stock. One of these, No 4786, is seen on 18 August 1954. An oil can resting on the tank outside the cab window, a headlamp, and a painted reporting No W10 show that it was still at work. *Brian Morrison*

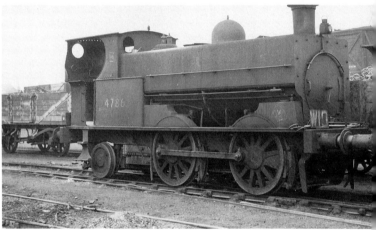

Further proof of the longevity of Crewe engines can be found in the *ABC* of 1947, which included details of the last of the 'Precursor' class 4-4-0s, No 25297 *Sirocco*, designed by Webb's successor, George Whale in 1904. I remember the last of the class at work on semi-fast and stopping trains down the North Wales coast during World War 2. They shared duties with the last of the 'George the Fifth' class 4-4-0s which were the work of Whale's successor, C. J. Bowen-Cooke. One of the class, No 5000 *Coronation* had marked another milestone when it came off works in 1911. It was named in honour of the Coronation of King George V and Queen Mary the year before.

Whale was only in office for six years from 1903, but Bowen-Cooke was CME for 11 years from 1909 to 1920, a period which included World War 1. H. P. M. Beames, appointed in November 1920, held the post for just over a

year because after the LNWR merged with the Lancashire & Yorkshire (LYR) from 1 January 1922, George Hughes the LYR CME headed the enlarged system due to his seniority.

A major post-Grouping change which took fresh work to Crewe was the closure of the North Staffordshire locomotive works at Stoke from 31 December 1926. Some staff were transferred to Derby, but most went to Crewe, which resulted in the introduction of workmen's trains from the Potteries to a platform inside the works.

It was built on the site of the old carriage sidings on the south side of the Chester line, close to where BR officially opened a new apprentices training school on 23 September 1955.

After Grouping, Beames continued at Crewe as Divisional Mechanical Engineer and masterminded a major works reorganisation. He also continued to live in the CME's house becoming

its last occupant. He is perhaps best remembered for his large and rather ungainly 0-8-4 shunting tanks of 1923.

The 6,000th locomotive, which did not appear until June 1930, was very different. It was a Horwich designed 'Hughes Crab', an inclined-cyclinder 2-6-0 of 1926: pure LMS. The 7,000th was pure British Railways — a Class 2, 2-6-2 mixed traffic tank no 41272, built in September 1950.

Not all of the 'numerical milestone' locomotives were among its most famous. The second *Coronation*, LMS No 6220 of June 1937 was perhaps the most striking, if not most dignified, of all, not solely those of Sir William Stanier who dominated the works between 1932 and 1944 when he was Chief Mechanical Engineer of the LMS.

Sir William took a great personal interest in machine tools and works practices, points stressed in the book *Crewe Locomotive Works and Its Men* by Brian Reed. It was published in 1982 shortly before the author's death. It is a

notable memorial to Brian Reed, a locomotive engineer who became a journalist.

World War 2 armament production in the town of Crewe was concentrated at the Rolls-Royce factory producing aero engines, rather than at the locomotive works, where the emphasis was on keeping locomotives in working order, although some armament work was done. It was in contrast to World War 1 when the works had been heavily engaged on a variety of munition manufacture and other work.

The works remained in LMS ownership until Nationalisation in 1948. Steam locomotive building continued for another decade. Initially the post-Nationalisation work had been concentrated on ex-LMS designs, such as the Class 2MT 2-6-2Ts and 2-6-0s, but Crewe was des-

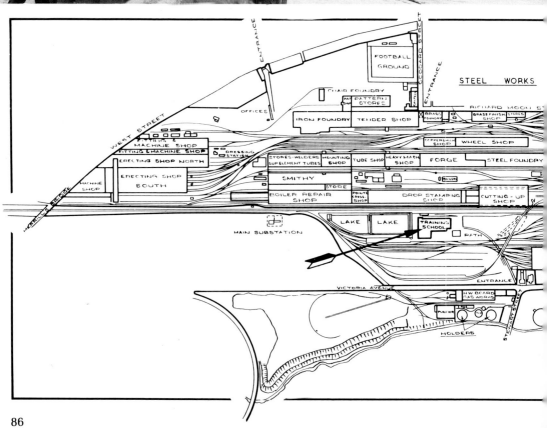

tined to build the first of the 999 BR standard locomotives, the 55-strong 'Britannia' class which appeared in 1951. Also built at Crewe was the unique Class 8P No 71000 *Duke of Gloucester*, which was completed in 1954. Steam locomotive production then turned to the Class 9F 2-10-0s, the last example of which to be built at Crewe, No 92250 completed nine days prior to Christmas 1958, was also the last steam locomotive constructed at the Works. Steam locomotive repairs ended early in 1967 when, appropriately, 'Britannia' class Pacific No 70013 *Oliver Cromwell* was ceremonially outshopped on 2 February, a cold and sunny winter's morning. It was the last of about 125,000 locomotives to have been repaired in 124 years. It was also the last steam locomotive to undergo a major overhaul on British Railways.

The switch to diesel and electric locomotive building began modestly in 1958 with a shunter, No 3419. In the 1960s production saw numerous main line diesels constructed. These included certain Type 2s (which later became Class 24) and Type 4s Nos D50-D137 (later Class 45); others of the class were built at Derby. Crewe also built, between 1961 and 1964, the bulk of the 'Western' class of diesel-hydraulics — Nos D1035-D1073 — and, following the completion of the last of that batch in December 1963, the Works also built Nos D1030-D1034 in place of Swindon. During the mid-1960s work was concentrated on the building of certain Type 4s (later Class 47). In 1972 Crewe built the two prototype High Speed Train power cars (Nos 41001 and 41002) and, following the success of the units on test (including a run in July 1973 when

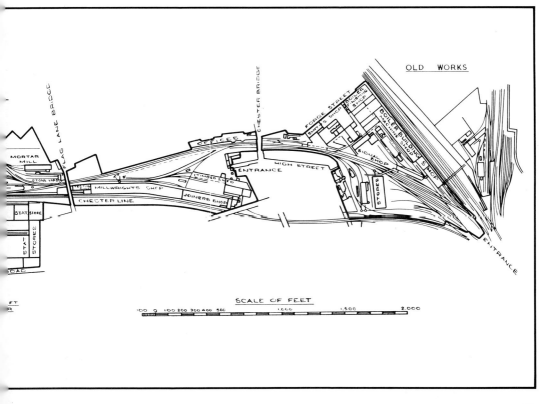

SCALE OF FEET

Right:
The 'Britannia' 4-6-2s were the first of 12 BR standard classes. The Class 9F 2-10-0s, introduced in 1954, were the last. The class was large: 251 were built of which a number were fitted with Crosti boilers. They included No 92020 in the middle of a row of the class under repair on 14 August 1963. *Rodney Wildsmith*

Below right:
After their introduction in 1951, the 55 locomotives of the 'Britannia' class were often to be seen at their birthplace. In February 1965, No 70035 *Rudyard Kipling* was under heavy repair. Only two years later, a sister engine, No 70013 *Oliver Cromwell* was the last steam locomotive to be repaired in the works. *P. L. Simpson*

Below:
Nearly 700 Stanier tapered-boiler Class 8F 2-8-0s were built from 1935. One of the later locomotives, No 48607, was noted with a newly painted boiler, on 7 February 1965. The notice board (left) is headed 'National Industrial Safety Month'. *P. L. Simpson*

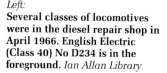

they reached 133mph, a trip on which the author was privileged to travel), an order was placed for 197 HST (InterCity 125) power cars — Nos 43002-198. Ordered in 1973, work started in 1974 and the first production power car, for the Western Region, was delivered in 1976 and work continued until 1982. Although Crewe constructed the power cars, the passenger coaches were constructed at Derby. The 8,000th production was a Class 43 InterCity 125 power car built in January 1978.

Crewe's final main line diesel work was inherited from Doncaster, when in 1983, the latter works was diverted from Class 56 production to build the new Class 58s. A total of 20 of the class, Nos 56116-135, was built at Crewe between 1983 and 1984.

Eleven years after the impressive HST record run the author broke his personal speed record on an APT run between Preston and Euston in 1984 which touched 138mph. This was still well below its originally projected maximum speed in West Coast main line operation of 155mph. The following week it was announced that the project had been scrapped.

Economies since Nationalisation led to a succession of redundancies until today the workforce is about 1,300 compared with some 10,000 workers during World War 1. The size of the works has been progressively reduced to some 80 acres — some 60 acres less than in its heyday.

After economies between 1962 and 1967, the offices built to the curvature of the original Chester line were left isolated, more than a mile from the main works buildings. In the 1970s they were replaced by a three storey, squat and square office block inside the main entrance in West Street. It is at the opposite side of the works to the Chester line, where an electrified

Watch out !
There's an APT about on the West Coast Main Line

Things you need to know

⇌ InterCityAPT

Above:
A major order of the 1980s was the refurbishment of Class 20 Bo-Bo English Electric locomotives built between 1957-68. Work is in progress on 15 July 1984. *R. W. Cragg*

Right:
Electric and diesel locomotives side-by-side: Class 86 No 86007 being converted to Class 86/4 beside Class 56 No 56090 on 24 April 1987. *Brian Morrison*

Left:
A pocket-card warned staff that the Advanced Passenger Train would be running between Euston and Gretna at speeds of up to 125 mph from 28 January 1980. *Author's collection*

Below:
A new-style ticket for a memorable return from Preston to Euston on 9 April 1984. The tilt of the APT was obvious but not unpleasant. *Author's collection*

⇌ InterCityAPT

Coach	Seat	Departs	Euston 1632
A	Second Class Smoker	Date	9 MAR 1984

BR. 4571.

British Railways Board (M)

CREWE RAIL OPEN DAY

SUNDAY 19th APRIL 1970

C 7 0065

This ticket includes admission to CREWE RAIL DEPOT and 2nd class rail travel as advertised

Chester, Kidsgrove, Longport, Stafford or Stoke-on-Trent to **CREWE Wistaston Road and back.**

This souvenir ticket may be retained

see over.

Left:
Crewe Wistaston Road was a station that appeared only on souvenir tickets for works Open Days. This is a complimentary issue I regret I never used.
Author's collection

Right:
**Freshly out-shopped: Railfreight
locomotive No 37045 on
31 October 1987.** *Brian Morrison*

connection was installed so that electric locomotives no longer needed to be towed in and out by
diesels.

The office block is the headquarters of the
Crewe 'site' of the privatised company, ABB
Transportation Ltd. It was known as BREL Ltd
from privatisation in 1988 until the title was
changed on 2 September 1992 to end confusion
over the name BREL. ABB Transportation is
80% owned by the international group ASEA
Brown Boveri. The remaining 20% of shares
have been held by management and staff since
buy-out from BR.

The most recent locomotives built are
Class 90 and Class 91 electric locomotives. For
the Class 91s, BREL was sub-contractor to GEC,
which designed and made the hi-tech power
units. In the spring of 1992 the works began a
three-year contract, worth £6 million, to repair
turbo-chargers of BR locomotives.

The works still hold the power to fascinate as
they prove on occasional Open Days. They
attract thousands of people and raise thousands
of pounds for charities. Locomotive arrivals and
departures are closely followed. Some years ago
when two ex-works diesel locomotives coupled
together passed through the station, two young
schoolboys told the staff they had been renum-
bered wrongly. They were not believed until an
inspector had second thoughts. His check
proved the boys right!

Below:
**Where locomotives came to end their days. Four
English Electric Class 40s in Stone Bank scrapyard,
Crewe: Nos 40044, 40057, 40058 (left). No 40195
(right) await their fate on 9 April 1987.** *Brian
Morrison*

10 Steam Sheds and Traction Depots

'Owing to the central position which Crewe occupies it is found advantageous to work most of the principal mail express and goods trains from this station, over various parts of the system.'

To do this, readers of the bulky, pocket-sized *Tourists' Picturesque Guide to the L &NWR* were told in 1876, there were about 550 engine drivers, firemen and others at Crewe locomotive sheds. About 120 locomotives were in steam daily 'for the stabling of which suitable sheds are provided; they cover an area of nearly two and a half acres'.

These sheds were successors to a small timber shed which the Grand Junction had built in 1839. That was at a time when a spare engine was kept always ready for use — throughout the night if necessary — with one of its duties being to act as 'banker' on the gradient towards Madeley.

Despite its junctions, Crewe did not become an important locomotive centre until after the retirement in 1857 of Francis Trevithick, son of the notable Cornish pioneer, who was the first

Below:
North shed 1892 with a variety of 'singles' and 2-4-0s outside the hipped-roof building. Webb three-cyclinder compound No 1311 *Celtic* is nearest the camera. *Jim Peden collection*

locomotive superintendent of the LNWR's Northern Division, based at Crewe. He kept few locomotives there, preferring to station them at other traffic centres — such as Rugby, Chester and Holyhead. Stafford was the main engine changing point as it formed the boundary between Southern and Northern divisions until they were amalgamated in 1862 by Trevithick's successor, John Ramsbottom.

Afterwards Crewe became the place for engine changing, but not everything happened at once because, when Ramsbottom took office, the sheds at Crewe could hold only 16 engines and employed only 64 people. Expansion began when an eight-road shed was opened in the late 1850s alongside the main line by the station. This was the first phase of the complex that later became known as Crewe North. It was followed by a 12-road shed opened in 1865, which became known as the Middle Shed and the best known of the group. It was equipped for heavy repair work as well as maintenance.

Only three years elapsed before a shed of similar size was constructed alongside it. This new shed was built partly around the Queen's Hotel, the company being either unable or unwilling to acquire the site. It opened in summer 1868 about the same time as the Chester line deviation, which ran across the mouth of the sheds and provided access to them.

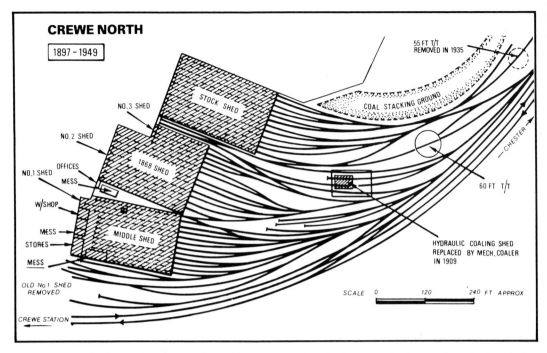

CREWE NORTH

1897 - 1949

NO.3 SHED

STOCK SHED

NO.2 SHED

NO.1 SHED   OFFICES

1868 SHED

MESS

W/SHOP

MESS

STORES

MIDDLE SHED

MESS

OLD No.1 SHED
REMOVED

CREWE STATION

55 FT T/T
REMOVED IN 1935

COAL STACKING GROUND

CHESTER

60 FT T/T

HYDRAULIC COALING SHED
REPLACED BY MECH. COALER
IN 1909

SCALE   0   120   240 FT APPROX

The 1868 shed was known as the 'Abba' or 'Abyssinia'. Change and development were continuous. Part of one of the original sheds was demolished for station expansion in the late 1870s, with the building of what became the middle of the three island platforms (Nos 6-11 of today). A third large locomotive shed, farthest from the main line, was built in the early 1890s. Known as the Stock Shed, it was different in character than the earlier sheds, being used almost entirely for locomotives waiting the call to the main works or those recently built awaiting allocation to other sheds.

The sheds gave off plenty of smoke but, being single-storey buildings, they never dominated the skyline. However, in 1909, a tall and ugly coaling plant, notable as the first in Britain to be completely mechanised, was built in the middle of the shed roads. This was an eyesore visible from much of the town. It was able to feed four

Below:
Abba shed lies behind 'Pacific' No 6229 *Duchess of Hamilton* with the Stock shed behind front buffers. The locomotive is in shining red livery and the date is probably autumn 1938. *Ian Allan Library*

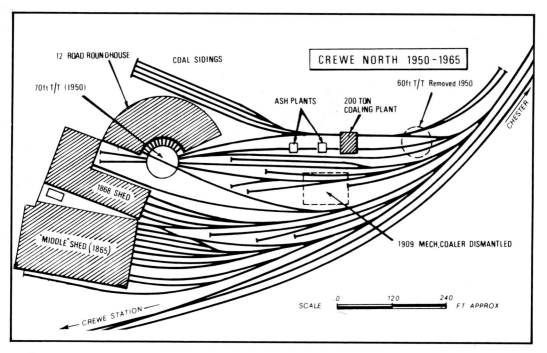

12 ROAD ROUNDHOUSE   COAL SIDINGS

CREWE NORTH 1950-1965

70ft T/T (1950)

60ft T/T Removed 1950

ASH PLANTS   200 TON COALING PLANT

CHESTER

1868 SHED

'MIDDLE' SHED (1865)

1909 MECH. COALER DISMANTLED

CREWE STATION

SCALE   .0   120   240   FT APPROX

tenders at once with coal hoisted to the over-head bunker by skip, rather than by railway wagon. There was an underground bunker as well, the whole complex being able to store 300 tons of coal.

The coaling stage was replaced early in BR days as the final modernisation of the sheds began. Its replacement was partially due to the need to provide a greater working space between the tracks as it had become difficult to carry out maintenance of locomotives, since these were becoming much larger than those running when the sheds were originally built.

Improvements planned by the LMS passed to BR undone and never quite came to fruition after Nationalisation partly due to lack of finance and partly due to the imminent intro-duction of diesel (and later electric) traction. Despite this a 70ft turntable was installed in 1950 and a 14-road semi-roundhouse was con-structed. These both occupied the site of the for-mer Stock Shed and part of the site of 'Abba'.

Crewe North sheds closed officially on 24 May 1965, but limited repair work continued at the site until the autumn. The sheds were quickly demolished and the site was later rede-

Left:
British Railways inherited run-down sheds. Improvements included a 70ft turntable on which No 46200 *The Princess Royal* is turning. The primitive lighting posts contrast to the electrification gantries in background (right). *J. R. Carter*

veloped as a large and much-used car-park. Also built on part of the site is the modern Signalling Centre. This appears almost 'lost' amid a waste land where thousands of steam locomotives built 'just across the road' once raised steam to pull generously-timed local trains to Chester or tightly-timed expresses across the border.

Allan Bakor, a former apprentice at Crewe North, paid tribute to the men of Crewe North in his book *Crewe Sheds*. He wrote:

'Crewe North men can justifiably claim to have worked the toughest footplate job ever regularly assigned in this country, for they worked the nightly sleeping car and mail trains between

Above:
BR demolished part of Abba shed to make way for two roundhouses of square outline. Caprotti fitted 'Black Five' No 44757 stands on the Abba site which backed on to rows of terraced railway houses, 20 August 1955. They were later demolished. *Brian Morrison*

Below.
A Hornby Dublo model of No 46232 *Duchess of Montrose* **is in my lounge as a reminder of the majesty and power of steam. On the same day as the 'Black Five' stood on the Abba shed site, the 'Duchess' simmered inside the dilapidated Middle shed, where roof and wall windows were broken. A memorable study by Brian Morrison**

Crewe and Perth — which were double-home jobs — two trains each way every night, 296 miles and with around 600 tons behind the tender. That this could be achieved night in night out was in no small measure because the locomotives were kept in first class condition by the maintenance staff, and with these and other achievements, Crewe North can fairly claim to have been the premier locomotive shed on the "Premier Line", not only in LNWR days, but subsequently under LMS and BR auspices too.'

Crewe South Shed

The famous footbridge across the mouth of the North junctions was a grandstand from which generations of enthusiasts were able to see some movements on and off North shed. But South shed was virtually inaccessible for it lay in a hollow sandwiched between the West Coast main line and the Independent Lines, being built as an integral part of the expansion of the 1890s.

The shed, of standard LNWR 12-road design, differed from the North sheds in having access from both ends. Its opening on 1 October 1897 changed the character of the locomotive scene by segregating passenger and goods engines — the former remaining at the original sheds, which then became Crewe North. Crewe South was coded 15S by the LNWR.

The new shed eased congestion through the station because locomotives working trains in and out of Basford Hall and Yard shunters no longer shuttled to North shed for servicing. But some exchanges continued to delight spotters, the LMS *Sectional Appendix* stating: 'Not more than eight dead engines, coupled together, may be conveyed between the North and South sheds and Crewe Engine Works provided a fireman travels on the rear dead engine and the handbrake on that engine is workable.'

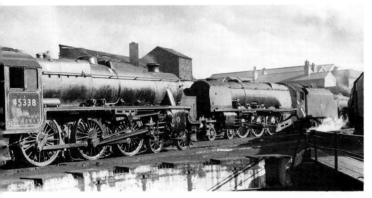

Above left:
A shed study on 28 August 1964 with Crewe still a locomotive changing point for a number of routes. By then electrification had reached Manchester, Liverpool and Stafford. 'Pacific' No 46239 *City of Chester* stands on a road adjacent to 'Black Five' No 45338. *J. R. Carter*

Left:
Three types of material, including slates, have been used to patch a roof which was itself a replacement for the original one. 'Pacific' No 46254 *City of Stoke-on-Trent* is about to leave its parent shed. *J. R. Carter*

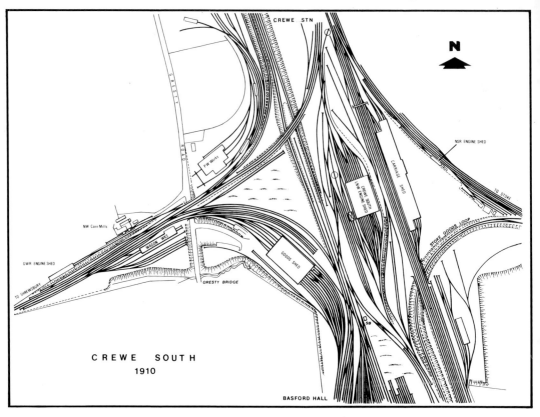

CREWE SOUTH
1910

The South shed approaches were generous and included separate lines to Basford Hall Junction to keep light engines clear of goods lines. The lines lay between the large fan of Up sidings and the Stoke goods lines, mostly in cutting at a slightly lower level.

Both sheds had allocations of just over 100 engines, although North shed had the wider variety and the more glamorous locomotives. But South shed had more visitors and was used by GWR locomotives working from the West Midlands and Shrewsbury after the closure of the ex-GWR shed in 1963. GWR engines, as well as those of the Cambrian before the Grouping in 1923, had used North shed regularly. In 1920 a mechanical coaling plant was established at the shed; this was probably the first such plant in Britain to be constructed out of concrete.

In 1946 South shed was selected as one location for an oil-firing scheme under which a

Left:
Crewe South, opened 1897, was a standard LNWR 12-road shed open at both ends. It was built for locomotives using the new Basford Hall yards. Webb four-cylinder compound 0-8-0 No 1282 is preparing to leave.
E. Mason

Right:
A number of modern BR classes were to be seen on shed in the final years before closure late in 1967. Third from left is 'Britannia' Pacific No 70012 *John of Gaunt*. The coaling plant is far left. Eight of the roads were re-roofed.
J. S. Hancock

Below right:
'Britannia' No 70022 *Tornado* had lost its nameplates while that of No 70025 *Western Star* was a crude replacement. The date is 15 May 1966. *Kevin Hughes*

significant number of steam locomotives were to be fitted with oil-firing equipment to reduce the need for the use of scarce coal. However, although the oil tanks were installed, the whole scheme was abandoned in September 1947. Until the new diesel depot was opened, Crewe South retained an allocation of diesel shunters and even after the completion of the new depot fuelling facilities were retained on the old site. In 1959 the shed roof over eight roads was replaced by one constructed of corrugated iron; the remaining four roads were left roofless and remained in that condition until closure.

Crewe South outlived North and at the latter's closure North's work was transferred to it. Until June and October 1965 a certain amount of maintenance continued at North shed, but by the end of that period South could handle all the work on the remaining steam fleet. South was not closed officially until 6 November 1967. At closure it had an official allocation of just six locomotives: one 'Black 5' and five '8Fs' which were used on workings to two collieries (Silverdale and Holditch).

Three preserved locomotives ('A4' No 4498, '4MT' No 75029 and '9F' No 92203) remained based at the shed until March 1968. The last steam locomotive to visit Crewe South was No 70013 *Oliver Cromwell* on 4 April 1968. Even after closure, diesels continued to be stabled in the shed, although the signing-on point was transferred to the station.

It was demolished a few days before the last steam locomotive to visit the area — 'Britannia' class No 70013 — became one of the locomotives that hauled BR's last official steam special in August 1968.

Crewe North Staffordshire Shed

A single-track 100ft-long NSR structure was opened in 1871, at a cost of £460, beside the tall North Staffordshire Sidings box and within sight of the West Coast main line. As it had no public road access, enginemen and staff had to cross the Kidsgrove tracks to reach it.

Locomotives took water from a tank at the southern mouth of the NSR Up sidings, which lay immediately opposite. LNWR track plans showed two small buildings, probably an office and a store, attached to the interior wall of the single-ended shed. A line alongside led to the Down sidings and a shunt back into a small wagon works and the interior tracks of two sheds. They were beside the Stoke Goods Loops into Basford Hall yard, close to the junction with the Kidsgrove branch. It is not clear why the NSR needed a locomotive shed at Crewe, for it was too small to service all the company locomotives that worked to or through Crewe. The locomotives used could easily have been serviced at North shed, for example. The answer may lie in the NSR's relationships with Euston, which were sometimes strained. At such times the NSR would want to assert its independence. Grouping took the shed into LMS ownership and it was closed within weeks — officially from 30 March 1923 — when the men were transferred to Crewe North. After closure the watering facilities at the site were retained.

Apart from the Crewe sheds there were four others in the group — Stafford (5C), Stoke (5D), Alsager (5E) and Uttoxeter (5F). Whitchurch was a sub-shed of Crewe North, with Cambrian and GWR engines stabled there.

Crewe Great Western Shed

The GWR shed at Gresty Lane was built by the LNWR to the traditional LNWR style and was located adjacent to the line to Nantwich. The shed was leased to the GWR, which opened it in 1870, about three years after the completion of the Wellington-Nantwich route. The original two road shed, a sub-shed of Wellington, could accommodate four locomotives, was extended in 1910 to service up to eight locomotives and, although its allocation was generally less than

Above:
Although the GWR and later the Western Region had their own small shed, their locomotives also used North and South sheds. 'Pacific' No 46238 *City of Carlisle*, **shedded there, prepares to leave North shed. Just ahead of it, waiting to join the Chester line, is a GWR 'Manor' class 4-6-0 on 25 June 1964.** *J. R. Carter*

Above right:
Easier to see, harder to identify: diesel locomotives of several classes are pictured at Crewe Diesel Depot on 22 December 1983, for which the south end of platforms provide a grandstand. Far left are two electric locomotives. The roof of the carriage shed on the Up side beyond the Stoke line, is in the middle background. *M. H. C. Baker*

Right:
The Diesel Depot, south end: the run-round road is far left and is seen on 28 April 1984. *M. G. Photographic*

that figure, there were usually several GWR visiting engines there.

The shed was tucked away on the Down side below the Shrewsbury line west of Crewe and had a similar air of remoteness to that of the NSR shed.

Access to the shed was controlled by the LNWR Gresty Lane No 1 box, to which drivers

were instructed to whistle on leaving the shed. The GWR Service Time Table Appendix of 1913 stated that locomotives were not to move forward until they were being hand signalled from the box. If it was foggy or snowing, firemen had to go to the box for instructions.

As a sub-shed of Wellington, Crewe Gresty Lane used the shed code 'WLN' in GWR days and became 84H on Nationalisation. On 14 April 1953 the shed was transferred to the London Midland Region, becoming a sub-shed of Crewe North (5A). It continued to provide the motive power for the Market Drayton branch until the line's closure. The shed closed on 17 June 1963 and was demolished soon after.

Diesel Depot

Euston-North Wales expresses follow an historically fascinating route through Crewe. They pass the site of South and North steam sheds, the diesel and electric depots and skirt the locomotive works and the Heritage Centre.

The Diesel depot is close enough to the south end of Platform No 1 for enthusiasts to see locomotives stabled in sidings between the main building and the main line.

Before depot construction could begin, a large mound of historic spoil, which had been banked above the main cutting during the 'Big Dig' of the Independent Lines, had to be cleared and taken to a railway tip at Betley Road.

Born in an age of transition, it was originally designed for the 'concentration' of steam locomotives from sheds in the Crewe Motive Power District needing periodic examination and heavy repairs and to segregate them from those on

shed for everyday servicing. It was also to be the base of the Basford Hall yard diesel fleet, which had, up to that point, been maintained amidst the smoky gloom of South shed.

But, during construction, policy changed and the depot was adapted for the maintenance of main line diesel locomotives and multiple-units, which were then slowly coming into service. The depot has five long through roads with three shorter bays at the south end and two at the north designed for the shunters.

When it opened late in 1957 it was officially designated as 'Crewe Diesel and Locomotive Examination Depot'. Among later improvements was the provision of another access road in the 1960s. Running behind the west side of the station, it links a run-round road outside the depot with the Up Chester Independent Line to the north.

Diesel multiple-units (DMUs) were operating in Crewe before the depot's completion so fuel and maintenance facilities were installed in the old LNWR carriage sheds on the Up side of the main line. The British Railways Productivity Council was told on 26 October 1956 that improvement work had started at Crewe while a similar project at Longsight carriage sheds, Manchester, was 'well in hand'. About the same time, a contract was let for the building of a staff amenity block at Crewe Shed.

Since opening, the Diesel depot at Crewe — which became 'CD' under the reclassification scheme of the mid-1970s — has played host to many of the diesel classes associated with the West Coast main line and the route towards Holyhead. In 1968, for example, the Stoke-on-Trent Division — at the time the London Midland Region allocated locomotives by Division rather than shed — was allocated 20 Class 40s, all 50 Class 50s, 75 Class 47s, 90 Class 24s and 47 shunters of various types. The Class 50s would have operated widely on West Coast main line services northwards, although, with the electrification of the route into Scotland, the class was destined to be transferred shortly to the Western Region. The depot was also destined to retain the last Class 24s in regular service. The depot also became synonymous with the Class 25 towards the end of the type's life. The shed was also the last depot of the prototype Class 40, No 200 (40122), which was eventually preserved on withdrawal.

The facilities of the shed have remained fairly constant although a new washing plant was commissioned on 21 December 1970. An Atlas wheel-turning lathe has been removed, and this allowed for the installation of a third jacking pad so that three locomotives can now be lifted at one time.

Electric Traction Depot

Part of the seven-acre site of the former LNWR carriage workshops, sheds and yard beside the Chester line opposite the locomotive works and a mile from the station provided a spacious site for the new Electric Traction Depot.

The LMS had closed the carriage workshops in 1932 but it was not until after World War 2 that part of the site was redeveloped for the Locomotive Works Apprentice School of 1955 (see Chapter 9). Two years later an electrification depot for BICC Ltd was completed and work started on the Traction Depot in 1959.

The main feature of the new Electric depot was an open-ended four-road shed with two-storey office block. It was designed to handle about 80 locomotives and half that number of EMUs.

Through roads were built to service four-coach sets — Class AM4, later Class 304 — which inaugurated the Manchester and Liverpool local services. Those units of the class which remain in service — now reduced to three-car sets — have been maintained at Longsight since 1987.

Originally the area was dominated by a single line which climbed across the mouth of the old works site and crossed Eagle Bridge into the works. The bridge was demolished in the 1980s after the electrified spur was constructed into the works off the Chester line. East and west facing lines run in and out of the Traction Depot from the Chester line.

Changes in motive power organisation led to the creation of Divisional Maintenance Engineers with support organisations at the headquarters of local traffic divisions which, for Crewe, was located at Stoke-on-Trent. There was a certain irony in Crewe now being controlled from Stoke-on-Trent, formerly the headquarters of the North Staffordshire. As Allan Baker and Gavin Morrison noted in *Crewe Sheds* 'In its day, the LNWR had employed as many men at Crewe as the NSR had employed on its entire system'.

There was serious concern among staff at the Electric depot in 1987 when it lost its allocation of the ageing Class 85s and was listed for closure with the loss of 80 jobs. The staff replied by making their own case for retention. 'We weren't prepared just to sit back and accept closure. We have a lot of expertise here which would have been lost forever,' the Depot engineer, George Alcroft, said afterwards.

Railnews, the BR staff newspaper, later reported that the depot had been reprieved after a review of freight traction requirements and by the allocation of additional locomotives to the depot.

Electric Control Room

Incorporated into the Electric depot is the electricity control room, which monitors the supply to the overhead equipment on the main line south to Rugeley, Colwich-Cheadle Hulme, and Crewe-Manchester/Liverpool. It also controlled the supply to the Manchester-Bury line at the different voltage of 1,200V dc — until its closure on 24 December 1991 for conversion to form part of the Manchester Metrolink project.

Left:
A departure from traditional shed and depot design was the provision of two bays for handling a specific type of locomotive. The bays are equipped for servicing small shunters. *British Railways*

11 Locomotives

When Crewe Works turned out a half-cab 2-4-0 passenger tank as its 2,000th locomotive in May 1876, the LNWR had a stock of 2,205 locomotives. They were estimated to run more than 40 million miles a year. Because they were built in fascinating variety, when recalling the company's locomotives, it is to be regretted that so few have been preserved. How much richer the preserved locomotive scene would be if at least one of the 4-4-0s still running after World War 2 could be admired today. So we have to be content with a small selection of locomotives, including 'Coal Tank' No 1054, a product of 1888 which was operational for some 70 years. Now housed in the Heritage Centre, a centre created on part of the Works' site, is 2-2-2 *Cornwall*, a Francis Trevithick design of 1847 with 8ft 6in driving wheels. *Cornwall* — Crewe locomotive No 75 — is not the Works' oldest surviving locomotive. That honour belongs to another in the National Collection: GJR No 49 *Columbine*. It is preserved in the form in which it was withdrawn in 1902 — a notable example of a type which influenced British locomotive design for more than four decades.

Amongst the most famous products of Crewe — and one that has been seen regularly on the main line since the return to steam in 1971 — is the 'Precedent' class 2-4-0 No 790 *Hardwicke*, which first ran again in 1975. It was built in 1872, although the present locomotive is a virtual rebuild of 20 years later.

In 1975, as part of the preparations for the Stockton & Darlington 150th anniversary celebrations, the locomotive was restored to operational condition after 45 years and made a memorable test run along the Cumbria coast on a rainy summer's day pulling Great Eastern director's saloon No 1.

Hardwicke made its name during the 1895 Railway Races to the North. It was among the host of Crewe-designed passenger and goods locomotives that graced the West Coast main line until the Grouping, under LNWR owner-

Below:
The first locomotive built at Crewe was Trevithick's 'single' *Columbine* of 1845. It is now preserved in the National Collection at York. *Ian Allan Library*

Right:
The second class of locomotives designed by John Ramsbottom were 7ft 6in 'singles' of the 'Problem' class. The locomotives later became better known as members of the LNWR's 'Lady of the Lake' class after one was shown at the International Exhibition of 1862 — the year in which No 762 *Locke* was photographed at Crewe. It is in the form in which it was first rebuilt. The class reached a total of 60 locomotives before building ceased in 1865.
Bucknall collection

ship, and was in LMS service until withdrawn for preservation in January 1932.

In contrast to the multi-coloured electric and diesel locomotives which run past Crewe today, the locomotives of the LNWR — exemplified by *Cornwall* displayed in 'The Railway Age' — were largely painted in a dignified gloss black picked out with narrow red and white stripes — a livery which dominated the station scene at Crewe for many decades.

The 2-2-2 wheel arrangement continued to be favoured by Ramsbottom when he became locomotive superintendent. Such a wheel arrangement was adopted for his famous 'Problem' class. But Ramsbottom is today best remembered for his 'DX' 0-6-0 goods locomotives, of which Crewe built more than 1,000 from 1858 onwards. A total of 86 were also constructed for the Lancashire & Yorkshire Railway. The 2-4-0 wheel arrangement had begun to replace the 2-2-2 by the time that Ramsbottom retired and

Below:
Webb's compounds and their achievements and failures are still talked about by enthusiasts today. Their long boilers and short cabs caused a stir when the 'Greater Britain' class was introduced in the early 1890s. No 525 *Princess May* is seen at Crewe in 1894.
Bucknall collection

Right:

The LNWR celebrated Queen Victoria's Diamond Jubilee in 1897 by painting 'Greater Britain' class No 2054 *Queen Empress* **in striking livery of creamy white and mauve with lined boiler bands and white tyres. The Royal Coat of Arms was placed on the rear driving splasher. The locomotive is seen at Crewe.** *Bucknall collection*

Below right:

One of Webb's later designs was four-cylinder compound 4-4-0s of the 'Alfred the Great' class. No 1957 *Orion* **at Crewe in 1902, the year before Webb was succeeded by George Whale.** *Orion* **was fitted with modified valve gear and a larger cab.** *Bucknall collection*

Bottom right:

When Whale succeeded Webb there was an urgent need to replace the compounds with more reliable and powerful locomotives and his design was of 'Precursor' class 4-4-0s and 110 were built in two years and a superheated version formed the 'George the Fifth' class, introduced by Whale's successor, C. J. Bowen Cooke in 1910. LMS No 5365 *Racehorse* **at Crewe in the early 1930s before '2' was prefixed to the number of the surviving engines of the class.** *Barry Thomas*

was succeeded by Francis Webb in 1871. Webb's 32-year reign as Chief Mechanical Engineer included production of a series of Compound classes, which ultimately comprised more than 300 locomotives. All got a reputation for being troublesome but, in contrast, Webb also designed superb classes of 2-4-0s and 0-6-0s, as well as 0-6-2Ts. The only two Webb-designed locomotives to survive are *Hardwicke* and the 'Coal Tank'.

Time recorders often used the 10½-mile climb to Whitmore and the easier five miles north to Minshull Vernon to compare the performances of different express locomotive classes.

The sharp curves at North Junction prevented speedy departures to Chester and Manchester. Yet the long, heavy and often double-headed Holyhead expresses must have looked a majestic sight as they pounded towards the North Wales coast.

Double-heading was begun in LNWR days — a reflection of the small engines policy adopted by the railway's Chief Mechanical Engineers — and was continued into LMS days. Such workings could produce several combinations: a Webb simplified Compound 4-4-0 piloting a 'Prince of Wales' 4-6-0; and an 'Experiment' 4-6-0 coupled ahead of a 'Claughton' 4-6-0 on a 16-coach Up day Irish Mail', which was illustrated in a memorable article by D. S. M. Barrie in the *Trains Annual* 1955. While the larger LNWR 4-6-0s were gradually displaced by 'Royal

Scots' on Holyhead expresses, LNWR 4-4-0s were still working along the coast during World War 2, often on trains stopping at now-forgotten stations.

Apart from the ex-NSR line to Stoke-on-Trent, every type of LNWR and LMS express locomotive worked over the lines radiating from Crewe. Grouping in 1923 brought a few outsiders: Hughes 4-6-0s and Aspinall Atlantics from the Lancashire & Yorkshire. The latter, a type almost completely foreign to Crewe, were unpopular with local enginemen.

Six driving wheel designs were considered better for working over Shap, yet after the LMS took control Midland Compound 4-4-0s were introduced on some Anglo-Scottish expresses. They went through Crewe on the middle road with the 'Royal Scot' when it was timetabled to run Euston-Carnforth non-stop. The 'Compounds' were generally used only on the Edinburgh expresses, since these were normally lighter than the services to Glasgow.

A number of 'Compounds' — of both pre and post-Grouping date — were still allocated to Crewe North shed in November 1950 and others were allocated to Chester. But these were, by this date, relics of an earlier age. During the late

Below:
In May 1911, 'George the Fifth' LNWR No 5000 *Coronation* became the 5,000th locomotive to be built at Crewe. *Bucknall collection*

1920s and 1930s, the appearance of various Fowler and Stanier designs — most notably the 'Royal Scots', the 'Jubilees', the 'Black 5s' and the Pacifics — displaced the earlier designs and completely revolutionised traffic patterns on the West Coast main line expresses.

The older types were, however, a long time in finally disappearing. The author remembers with delight finding the last of the 'Claughton' 4-6-0s — No 6004 — at Edge Hill shed in 1946. It was still in prewar LMS livery and was used for working local passenger and goods trains in the Liverpool area. Built in 1921 and rebuilt only seven years later, it survived until 1949, having outlived the rest of the class by eight years. As the last survivor, LMS rated 5XP, it had its own class entry in the *ABC of LMS Locomotives*.

The 'Claughton' was among 50 former LNWR locomotives still shedded at Edge Hill in 1946, although the return of peace brought a speed-up in their withdrawal. Visiting Crewe Works with fellow members of the British Locomotive Society on 14 July, I found the scrap line filled by representatives of several classes, all but one designed by Webb. The locomotives concerned

were No 6734 (a Webb 2-4-2T), No 6869 (an 0-6-2T), No 7934 (one of a class of 0-8-4Ts which H. P. M. Beames introduced in 1923), No 27484 (an 0-6-0ST), No 27605 (an 0-6-2T), Nos 28209, 28289 and 28303 (all 0-6-0s designed for coal traffic belonging to a class introduced by Webb in 1873).

In the Works on that day were the frames of two 'Pacifics' — No 6253 *City of St Albans* and No 6254 *City of Stoke-on-Trent*. Only about a dozen years later the Stanier Pacifics were relegated to main line freights after being displaced in steam's twilight years by English Electric Type 4 diesel-electrics.

Slower goods trains in the late 1950s were still being headed by veteran 0-8-0s, including the famous 'Super D' types derived from the original Webb design of 1892 and a major Whale rebuild of 1908. Some were allocated to Crewe South shed from its opening in 1897. One rea-

son they lasted so long was that a Fowler 0-8-0 design of 1929, intended to replace the older locomotives and similar locomotives from other LMS constituent companies, was not quite as successful as hoped. Construction of the Fowler design was restricted to only 175, compared with a total of more than 500 in the three LNWR classes. The Fowler design was to be seen mainly in Lancashire.

Right:
**The 'Cauliflowers' were
introduced four years after
Webb began building a class of
0-6-0 'coal engines' several of
which passed into BR
ownership. They weighed just
32 tons, four tons less than the
'Cauliflowers'. No 58323 is
tender-to-tender with an ex
Lancashire & Yorkshire 0-6-0.**
C. B. Golding

Below right:
**The Webb influence lingered
after Nationalisation. A Class 2F
0-6-0 'Coal Engine' No 58323,
survivor of an 1873 class, stands
in the works yard on
26 February 1950.** *H. Weston*

Below:
**A sight that always delighted a
works visitor: a freshly
repainted 'Pacific'. A chock is
wedged under the leading bogie
wheel of No 46238** *City of
Carlisle* **standing outside the
Paint Shop on 25 September
1955.** *D. McGarry*

As with so many LNWR engines, the 0-8-0s were at Crewe through both World Wars. But by the late 1940s the reign of the ex-LNWR types was coming to an end. In 1947 the LMS announced a locomotive standardisation policy, where 393 different classes of locomotive were to be replaced by a fleet of only 11 classes. Amongst wheel arrangements scheduled to disappear were 4-4-0 and 0-6-0 tender engines. In the event Nationalisation of the railways in 1948 meant that the LMS was never in a position to implement its policy, but its influence can be seen in the development of the BR 'Standards' in the 1950s. Ironically, however, both policies were ultimately to be supplanted by the Modernisation Plan of 1955 and many pre-Grouping designs were consequently to survive well into the 1960s.

Completing the Motive Power Picture: Locomotives of the GWR, Cambrian Railways and the North Staffordshire

The LNWR (and LMS) dominance of Crewe would have been complete but for the minor intrusions of three companies with which it had (generally) good relations — the GWR, the Cambrian and the North Staffordshire. One curious aspect was that all these three had right-hand

Above:
GWR 'Barnum' class 2-4-0 No 3216 pictured at Crewe about 1920. Right of the tender is a Cambrian Railways coach in all-green livery. *R. W. Miller collection*

drive locomotives, in contrast to the LNWR's left-hand drive policy.

The Shrewsbury route provided the approach for GWR locomotives from that town and from Wellington and, before Grouping, it also provided access for the Cambrian Railways via Whitchurch. The GWR was to provide the only double-framed locomotives seen at Crewe.

When the line to Market Drayton was opened in 1863, GWR locomotives appeared at Crewe for the first time. The earliest services were probably operated by the Wolverhampton-built 2-4-0s — such as '481' class introduced in 1869 — based either at Crewe or Wellington. The 2-4-0s of various classes continued to be seen at

Below:
Cambrian 4-4-0 No 94, as reboilered in 1920, awaits station signals. *W. H. Whitworth*

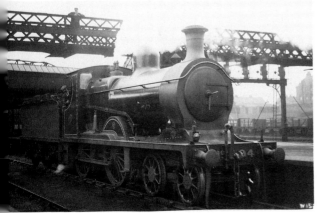

Crewe until the 1930s. Representatives of both the 'Stella' and 'Barnum' classes were to be regularly seen over the line. By the 1920s 4-4-0s were also to be seen and in 1921 there were four of the type allocated to Gresty Lane. These were 'Duke' class No 3267 *Cornishman* and 'Bulldog' class Nos 3314 *Mersey*, 3362 *Albert Brassey* and 3400 *Winnipeg*. The tender locomotives were replaced later by 2-6-2Ts of Class 51xx and by 0-6-0PTs, which were used on the branch pick-up goods.

Most GWR locomotives to the town were serviced at the company's small shed, which, at the Grouping, had an allocation of two 2-6-2Ts and an 0-6-0PT. But the GWR's locomotive presence at Crewe was much stronger. Other regular visitors at Crewe included the powerful Class 28xx 2-8-0s, which were used on the through freight services.

Locomotives of 37 GWR classes, ranging from 'Castle' class 4-6-0s to shunting tanks, were authorised to work over the Wellington route and to 'use' Crewe station, North shed and run round the triangle formed between Gresty No 1, Basford Hall Sorting Sidings North and Salop Goods Junction. GWR locomotives could also run into Basford Hall and Gresty Lane sidings. While operating over these metals, GWR locomotives were able to keep their ATC shoes in the operational position.

As noted in Chapter 3, LNWR passenger timetables included the Cambrian's main line services between Whitchurch and the coast, and the Cambrians' locomotives regularly worked through Whitchurch to Crewe. In Crewe the locomotives were serviced at North shed. During World War 1, Cambrian locomotives worked to Crewe over the Mid Wales Railway with 'Jellicoe Specials', which carried thousands of tons of Welsh steam coal on its journey towards the huge naval base at Scapa Flow in order to feed

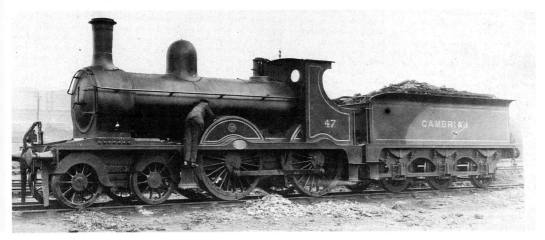

the hungry boilers of the Grand Fleet. And in 1917-18, the company loaned the LNWR 4-4-0s Nos 47 and 85 and 0-6-0 No 83 to help meet a locomotive shortage.

There were three strands to NSR traffic at Crewe: the Derby passenger service; traffic to the NSR Goods Yard; and the 'Llandudnos'. The company used a variety of locomotives on the Derby services and 0-6-2Ts and 0-6-0s on coal traffic. In 1907, John Henry Adams, who had become Locomotive Carriage & Wagon Superintendent five years earlier, built two 0-6-0s (Nos 82 and 83) at Stoke-on-Trent. These were quickly sent to the LNWR Edge Hill shed to work Liverpool-Burton on Trent/Derby goods trains. The summer North Wales service was the only one which the NSR did not operate with tanks — although some were occasionally used — and in 1910 four Adams-designed 4-4-0s (Nos 86, 87, 170 and 171) were built at Stoke Works specially for the service. The quartet could carry enough coal and water to make non-stop outward journeys from Stoke to Llandudno.

Modern Traction

The Crewe influence on diesel design has never been as strong as with steam but there was a progressive attitude to them in LMS days and diesel shunters were used in Basford Hall yards from the mid-1930s. They worked alongside 'Jinty' 0-6-0s; the latter were always known in Crewe as 'Humpies'.

The first of Britain's main line diesels — the attractive LMS pair Nos 10000 and 10001 — were of English Electric/Derby design and were based at Willesden. Seen regularly on West Coast main line services, the duo often received heavy maintenance at Crewe after the diesel depot was opened. Also in the late 1950s and early 1960s Crewe saw a trio of Bulleid-designed/English Electric-built 1Co-Co1 diesel-electrics, Nos 10201-3. These locomotives, which had been designed for the Southern Region and built between 1951 and 1954 were the forerunners of the English Electric Type 4 (later Class 40) diesel-electrics which became a common sight in the Crewe area later. The impression, gained from the author's experiences during cab runs with the Up 'Merseyside Express' (with a three-coach Southport portion) and later the Up 'Mancunian' was that the Type 4's were powerful and reliable, but not especially fast in acceleration.

With the introduction of the 1970 timetable Crewe diesel depot was allocated a complete class of more powerful English Electric Type 4s of 2,700hp. These 50 locomotives, which were originally leased to British Rail and had been based around Crewe from new in 1967-8, had been modified to speed up Anglo-Scottish expresses prior to the electrification of the route and operated in place of the older Type 4s. The completion of the electrification south of Crewe had made BR conscious of the contrast between the standards of service on the diesel and electric sections of the West Coast route and by modifying the Type 4s to operate in multiple, improved timings could be achieved. Becoming Class 50 under the TOPS scheme, the class was gradually transferred to the Western Region with the completion of the electrification of the route to Glasgow Central in 1974. The first went to Bristol in October 1972 and the last left the LMR by mid-1976.

Since electrification in the early 1960s, West Coast main line services have been worked by a

113

series of increasingly powerful classes of loco-motive. Whilst many of these were produced by outside builders, a number have also been con-structed by Crewe Works. The first locomotive specifically designed to operate at 25kV ac, No E3001, was handed over to BR by Associated Electrical Industries (AEI) at a ceremony at Sandbach on 27 November 1959.

The first generation of ac locomotive, classified 1-87 under the TOPS scheme, emerged between 1959 and 1973 and all became a regular sight at Crewe. Latterly, the earlier classes, 81-85, were most usually seen on freight services, with the passenger services being han-dled by Classes 86 and 87. The former were used largely on services to Manchester and Liv-erpool, whilst the Class 87s, introduced in 1973, were used on Anglo-Scottish services. A number of locomotives were allocated to Crewe Electric depot.

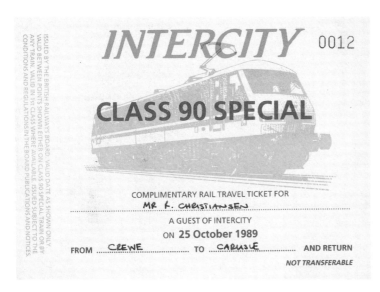

Above:
Servicing, including brake testing, and repainting being carried out on No 86211 in the works on 20 September 1975. *Brian Morrison*

Left:
Before being named *BBC North West* at Carlisle, Class 90 No 90015 hauled a demonstration train from Liverpool to Manchester Piccadilly via Crewe and then returned to reverse in Platform No 1 at Crewe before heading north for the ceremony. *Author's collection*

The latest generation of 110mph ac locomotives appeared in the late 1980s. These were the Class 90s, which were built between 1987 and 1988 — the first new ac locomotives for more than a decade. The Class 90s were built at Crewe and were followed through the Works by the Class 91s designed for use on the East Coast main line. Both classes used the same initial test route — the Down slow line between Crewe Coal Yard box and Winsford, which permitted running at up to 75mph. With the appearance of the Class 90s, most of the older ac locomotives, of Classes 81-85, were withdrawn, bringing yet another revolution to the Crewe locomotive scene.

Dieselisation of passenger services on Crewe's cross-country routes began several years ahead of main line electrification. One of the earliest was Crewe-Stoke-on-Trent-Derby in September 1957, when Birmingham Railway Carriage & Wagon three-car diesel multiple-units replaced the existing steam-hauled services.

These units, fitted with four engines giving a total of 600hp, enabled significant cuts in journey times to be made and, as elsewhere, led to a substantial increase in traffic. In 1961 passenger traffic over the line increased by 42 per cent. In keeping with the honoured North Staffordshire tradition, one daily train each way was extended down the North Wales coast to form a Derby-Llandudno service. But, unlike its predecessor, it ran all the year round and made frequent stops.

Above:
APTs made test runs on the West Coast main line in the early 1980s as well as operating a limited number of public-timetabled Euston-Glasgow services. Sets were allocated to Crewe Electric Traction Depot. A short set of five cars is seen waiting to return to the depot. *Chris Morrison*

Crewe-Holyhead services, and those between Manchester/Liverpool and Cardiff, via Shrewsbury, were worked with locomotive-hauled stock. The lines were, for many years, the haunt of the Classes 24 and 25 Bo-Bo diesel-electrics, although the BRCW Class 33s, normally based on the Southern Region, were also used on Crewe-Cardiff services for a short period. Local services on the routes towards Chester and Shrewsbury were DMU operated. The demise of the popular Type 2 diesels by the mid-1980s, along with the gradual withdrawal of the first-generation DMUs, has seen the new generation of multiple-unit appear on a wide range of services. In the 1990s, Class 158s are seen on certain services, whilst the local stopping trains between Crewe and Shrewsbury are now in the hands of the single-car Class 153s.

Through services from Euston to the North Wales coast are now normally provided by High Speed Train sets, whilst these units — with their Crewe-built power-cars — are also to be seen on InterCity services from the northwest and Scotland to the southwest; ironically, despite the electrification of the West Coast main line, these services operate over long stretches of the route with diesel traction.

Although this chapter has, inevitably, concentrated on passenger services through Crewe, the area also sees considerable freight traffic both running through the district and originating at a number of locations within it. The majority of freight and parcels services on the main line are electric-hauled, although the older generation of locomotive has, since the late 1980s, gradually been replaced by the new Class 90s in their new and varied Railfreight liveries. Diesel traction also survives, although again the earlier generation of locomotive — such as the Class 24s — has disappeared and been replaced by Class 47s and the more recent Class 56.

12 'The Railway Age' and Forgotten Railways

The nature of the ever-changing face of Crewe was reflected during a visit by the Queen and Prince Philip on 24 July 1987. For, as well as touring the BREL works and the Heritage Centre (which the Queen officially opened), the royal visitors also went to the Rolls-Royce car works and left the town by driving along a link road between the M6 motorway and Crewe and Nantwich, three days after the link had been opened.

The link enables Crewe Heritage Trust to advertise the Centre, now known as 'The Railway Age', as being 'just minutes from the M6'. It is a place of signal boxes, of contrasting designs and ages. A central attraction and vantage point is the North box. Rebuilt beside the Chester line are the old 'A' box, which once nestled under the station roof in a position almost within sight of its 'retirement' home, and the two-storey Exeter West box, which is now far from its original home. As well as restored steam and diesel locomotives on display, there is *Cornwall*. After the locomotive's withdrawal, the LNWR noted the veteran among 'objects' preserved from its early history.

In Edwardian days, the company stated that while its historic relics were being kept at Crewe, a 'museum is being arranged at Euston', adding with its usual pomp: 'This will be the first railway museum in the British Empire.'

A modern historic relic standing beside the West Coast main line on which it once ran, is the only surviving six-carriage APT-P (prototype Advanced Passenger Train), which was built at Derby and which was designed to revolutionise travel over the twisting West Coast route. Outside North signal box is a brick-walled ramp rising towards the upper floor. This is a remnant of the works' narrow gauge tramway to Spider Bridge spanning North Junction.

Crewe offers historically-minded and nostalgia-seeking visitors more than the Heritage Centre. The works have contracted, Eagle Bridge has been demolished and the village born of the Grand Junction has gone, but near Christ Church is a club which looks almost colonial at casual glance. It was founded by Bowen-Cooke

JULY 4th–AUGUST 16th

Above:
Crewe celebrated 150 years as a railway centre with a seven-week long Festival in summer 1987. It included the opening by the Queen of the Heritage Centre. A supermarket was subsequently built on part of the land which the Festival had used. On 11 July 1992 the Heritage Centre was relaunched as 'The Railway Age'. *Author*

as the LNWR Veterans' Club in 1919 as men were returning from World War 1.

Nearby, a furniture store and recently-constructed small office block occupy the trackbed of the original Chester main line leading to Chester Bridge in Edleston Road. Its low arch has been infilled but it is still topped by charming, ornate ironwork. Across the road is the site of the main works' offices, destroyed by fire some years ago.

A short walk away, within sight of the clock-tower-dominated town centre, are the preserved houses of workers and foremen. They add charm and character to an area of modern shops and offices.

My copy of Chaloner's history — acquired, I suspect after years on a library shelf — has a strong, musty smell. It is a strong reminder of the Crewe that I knew as a boy. But it cannot quite match a nostalgic blast of smoke from a preserved Stanier Pacific making a sure-footed start round North curve heading for Chester to storm under the city walls on its way to pound the coast and enchant many a holiday-maker and pensioner strolling along a North Wales promenade.

13 Crewe Today

Retired station staff can still remember when smoke and steam billowing along the platforms was so thick that they could not see the ends of them. Today, their successors can usually see expresses approaching from north and south along the West Coast main line when they are still over a mile away.

Crewe's steam image, glorious only to enthusiasts, was gradually blown away by the BR modernisation plan launched in the mid-1950s. As diesel and electric traction took over, staircases between the platforms and booking hall, which had been encased to act as ducts to carry steam clear of them, were opened out to reveal a brighter and cleaner station, although ensnared in a dense and ugly 25kV overhead wirescape.

That was symbolic of 'Britain's New Railway' being created between Euston the West Midlands and the Northwest. The Manchester and Liverpool routes were converted first and Crewe became their hub.

The wirescape was simplified as part of the 1985 multi-million pound modernisation programme. It improved amenities for passengers; signalling and track layout for operators and paved the way for modernisation of the West Coast main line.

A plan announced in June 1990 aimed to link London with Manchester and Liverpool in under two hours and Glasgow in under four, with IC 250 trains running up to 155mph (250km/h) from May 1994. 'As well as InterCity trains the line will, from 1993, be carrying international trains to Paris and Brussels,' stated InterCity.

But as recession deepened it became too costly a project and the £750 million rolling investment programme planned to continue into the next century was soon in difficulties. In summer 1992, BR told three large railway stock manufacturers competing for the main contract that it had lapsed and would not be reopened in the foreseeable future.

Below:
On 5 January 1987 Class 47 No 47449 heads past Betley Road, south of Crewe on the West Coast main line, with the 08.05 Portsmouth Harbour-Liverpool Lime Street service. *Paul Shannon*

Besides recession there was uncertainty surrounding Government privatisation plans and the need to replace ageing stock and infrastructures. Much electrical equipment on the Liverpool and Manchester lines is over 30 years old — several years more than that between Euston and the West Midlands and some 15 years older than masts and cabling between Weaver Junction and Glasgow, still in a satisfactory condition.

Under a revised West Coast modernisation programme of October 1992, more than £400 million — less than the cost of buying IC 250 trains — is being spent over 10 years renewing and upgrading track and signalling to raise maximum speeds from 110mph to 125mph.

Overhead and electrical equipment south of Warrington and in Greater Manchester will be renewed.

The revised programme was unveiled ahead of the Government privatisation plans. An early reaction came from a former member of the British Railways Board, Simon Jenkins. He con-

fessed in *The Times* in February 1993 that he was mystified at why the East Coast main line was to be privatised but not the West Coast. He described that as 'limping'.

Even though the West Coast lives to some extent under the shadow of its more glamorous rival, it remains busy and Crewe handles over 400 trains on its busiest days. Cross-country and local services form the majority, but well over 100 InterCity expresses run via Crewe, mainly on Anglo-Scottish routes and between Euston and Liverpool and, to a lesser extent, Manchester. Among them are well patronised 'Pullmans'. Services between Edinburgh and the South were speeded up after Edinburgh-Carstairs was electrified, though 'The Clansman', the day service which linked Crewe and Inverness, was cut back to Edinburgh when the East Coast scheme was completed.

Crewe lost its links with the Fylde coast when three daily Euston-Blackpool services were withdrawn in autumn 1992 and another InterCity route between Crewe and the seaside was pruned when the Euston-Holyhead HST service was reduced to three daily trains in the same year.

Yet despite changes, Crewe retains its romance and appeal and it is pleasant to recall Canon Roger Lloyd's thoughts in *The Fascination of Railways* written soon after Nationalisation: 'The railway lover counts no time wasted which he spends sauntering on a good station.' Part of Crewe's fascination can be experienced

Below:
One of the most heavily loaded Railfreight Distribution (RfD) European services is 6M86 08.50 Dover-Crewe. This feeds into connecting services to Northwest England, Scotland, North Wales, Yorkshire and Northeast England. Here, on 24 April 1992, the service is seen at Whitmore double-headed by Class 90s Nos 90140 and 90136. Note the variety of livery which is such a mark of the modern railway scene. *Paul Shannon*

Above:
The remaining stub of the ex-North Staffordshire Railway line from Market Drayton to Stoke serves Silverdale Colliery via a chord line constructed at Madeley. Silverdale Colliery was one of the coal mines deemed unprofitable at the end of 1992 amidst much controversy. In happier times, on 13 April 1988, Class 20s No 20113 and 20055 pause at Silverdale with empty MDVs for Holditch — the main flow from Holditch was to Llanwern with the trains staged at Basford Hall *en route* to Shrewsbury and South Wales — while HAAs are being loaded for a service to Ironbridge. *Paul Shannon*

when the sleeper expresses and Travelling Post Offices arrive by night and Royal Mail staff outnumber passengers.

Nowadays there is less time for the saunterer to relish the scene for trains do not stop as long as once they did. 'The Royal Highlander', which now runs to Fort William as well as its time-honoured terminus of Inverness, is booked to call for only three minutes — a third of its scheduled time 30 years ago.

Concentrating Scottish sleeper services on Euston led to the transfer from Kings Cross of 'The Aberdonian', now 'The Night Aberdonian',

which on the Down journey stops at Crewe soon after midnight.

West Coast Up and Down Postal Specials between Euston and Glasgow remain the backbone of the TPO services that meet and exchange mail at Crewe. Others include Manchester - Dover, for which Post Office staff line up waiting trolleys with military precision between Platforms Nos 1 and 5, and the Down Peterborough-Carlisle TPO which reaches Crewe via Leicester and Derby. Introduced by Royal Mail Letters in September 1991, the service is unusual because the Up Working is routed via Newcastle and York.

The passenger popularity of Class 158 trains and the scenic beauty of the Welsh Marches were among factors which led to some of the biggest ever changes made in Crewe's cross country services. From May 1993 the frequency of Manchester-Cardiff services, timetabled into HST connections at Newport, was almost doubled to hourly. The Shrewsbury-Newport Welsh Marches Line is promoted by Regional Railways in its *Britain's Scenic Railways* brochure, but ironically the time passengers have to enjoy the views has been reduced through raising much of the Crewe-Newport line limit to 90mph.

Twenty years ago, most Manchester-Cardiff journeys took 4½ hours — 90min more than today's fastest timings. Western Region Table 6 showed six weekday trains running only to Crewe where some connections added 1hr 40min to the Manchester leg.

The Heart of Wales Line — a beckoning, inspiring title for the old Central Wales Line — is Manchester-Cardiff timetable integrated with DMUs through to Crewe. In 1973, the timetable offered only tardy Shrewsbury connections with Crewe and Northwest services. Today, Heart of Wales single-car Class 153 trains maintain Crewe-Shrewsbury local services. They call at two stations within Crewe's boundaries since 1974: Nantwich and Wrenbury — the latter is possibly the borough's least known station.

Since the end of InterCity's Blackpool services, some holiday-makers have changed off Class 158-operated services from Cardiff at Stockport or Manchester Piccadilly, rather than at Crewe, and again at Preston. And, after the opening of Manchester Airport station 17 May 1993, a Friday night Cardiff train was extended to it. The £28 million Airport link from the Styal Line is the latest route to be reached from Crewe. If, as originally planned, a west to south spur is built to the Styal Line, direct services via Crewe are likely to be introduced.

Passenger totals on the Manchester-Cardiff and associated Liverpool service, have increased by 10% since Class 158s were introduced, but

The diversionary line from Sandbach to Northwich, via Middlewich, which lost its timetabled passenger services on 4 January 1960 was scheduled for closure as a through route in May 1992. On 2 May 1992, a week before the planned closure, the line is traversed by Class 31 No 31516 at Middlewich with an RfD (Chemicals) trip working conveying salt from Middlewich and caustic soda from Sandbach. In the event, closure did not place, with InterCity sponsoring the retention of the route. *Paul Shannon*

Regional Railways refuse to give figures because of competition associated with privatisation and coach and bus deregulation. Their stance is a good example of the changed climate in which BR operates for I remember when the first DMU services began in the 1950s, they were anxious to publicise almost every extra passenger carried.

Manchester and Cardiff are separated by 170 rail miles. Crewe's other Class 158 route, which was also given an hourly frequency in May 1993, stretches 105 miles to Holyhead, although most hourly trains turn round at Bangor (80 miles). Some that continue to Holyhead are extended south of Crewe. One destination is Birmingham International. Unlike Manchester-Cardiff, Regional Railways face strong road competition following multi-million pound improvements to the North Wales coast road.

Much of the route towards Holyhead has been upgraded for 90mph running and political pressure is growing for its electrification as it forms the main link between Ireland and the Continent through the Channel Tunnel.

Regional Railways electrified services to Liverpool Lime Street and Manchester Deansgate, the most intensive of Crewe's local services, will be improved by Class 323 trains expected in May 1994, a year behind schedule, to replace the 33-year old slam door Class 304s and more recently introduced Class 305s. Faster Manchester services will exploit line speed improvements, including the long stretch over the Sandbach embankment, where 75mph may be possible.

Among services to benefit will be the mail and parcel operations of Rail express systems, which has given Crewe a new landmark: a tall, multi-coloured sign between the station and Rail House. While signposting the entrance to the Traction Maintenance Depot, Training Centre and Parcels Point, it also helps strangers find the station entrance.

The biggest renaissance at Crewe in recent years has been in freight. It began with the return of wagonload traffic in 1991 after an absence of 19 years, and continued when Freightliners started using Basford Hall the following year. The yard quickly grew to become the hub of the Freightliner network and among the busiest in Britain.

Seen from expresses on the main line, the only and unsatisfactory grandstand, the thinned down network of sidings and running lines often look a little empty. But the picture is deceptive because long distance trains run non-stop through the Independent Lines or halt only briefly in the Yard. In contrast to loose-coupled wagon days when trains arrived and departed with traffic for a host of places including small country stations, Freightliners use only a few well defined routes. Many are shown on Yard Arrival and Departure sheets as running Monday-Friday while others feature only once or twice weekly. The 1993 pattern of Freightliner diagrams covered workings via Crewe of services between South and East Coast ports — Felixstowe, Harwich Parkeston Quay, Dover, Southampton and Tilbury — and terminals in Northwest England, Yorkshire and Scotland: Trafford Park, (Manchester), Seaforth and Garston (Liverpool), Wilton (Teesside) and Coatbridge near Motherwell.

Eire container traffic was transferred to Seaforth after the closure of Holyhead Freightliner Terminal in April 1991 and most is routed to and from Liverpool for exchanging at Crewe.

Another significant part of RfD traffic is carried in part train loads re-marshalled at Crewe, which also handles trainload freight, private company trains and BR departmental workings. Trainload freight workings including coal, steel, petroleum and aggregates are run to meet demand. Trains change crews at Basford Hall and wait if necessary for paths. Company traffic ranges from fertilisers to pet foods.

Not all freight is routed through the yard. Trains from Cheshire working to Cornwall run via the Independent Lines to Gresty Lane for a crew change. And some merry-go-round coal trains run through the middle roads of the station. Those between Silverdale Colliery at Newcastle-under-Lyme and Fiddler's Ferry power station, near Warrington, make a yard stop.

The opening of the Channel Tunnel will not have the impact on Crewe that local interests hoped, despite having land available for a freight terminal close to motorways. RfD is concentrating European container and other traffic at Seaforth and Trafford Park while Basford Hall will continue as a main centre for the sorting of Dover-Dunkerque train ferry traffic for much of Northern

A strong International presence at Crewe is provided by ABB Transportation Ltd as owners of the locomotive works which celebrate their 150th anniversary in 1993. Although the workforce is down to 1,300, there is a multi-million pound order book of contracts dating into the mid-1990s. Orders for the Equipment and Vehicle Repair Divisions, which the company has based at Crewe, do not include any for new locomotives and the Class 91s may pass into history as the last built there. In winter 1993, the company said they had no plans for locomotive construction, although equipment has been mothballed in case of future need. Meanwhile its policy of diversification is reflected in a current three year contract to overhaul and refurbish traction motors for NSE Classes 310, 312 and 315. The work will be done by the Equipment Division. The Vehicle Repair Division overhauls locomotives and stock and both divisions carry out work for the company's sites at Derby and York, including component manufacture for Class 465 Networkers.

Appendices

Appendix 1

Opening Dates of LNWR lines and Associated West Coast Companies

Line	Company	Date
Birmingham-Warrington	GJR	4 July 1837 Pass
		1 February 1838 Goods
London-Birmingham	L&B	17 September 1838 Pass
Chester-Crewe	GJR	1 October 1840
Sandbach-Crewe	M&B	10 August 1842
Carlisle-Edinburgh	Cal	15 February 1848
Harecastle (Kidsgrove)-Crewe	NSR	9 October 1848
Chester-Holyhead	LNWR	18 March 1850
Shrewsbury-Crewe	LNWR	1 September 1858
Sandbach-Northwich	LNWR	11 November 1867
Chester-Crewe: Works Deviation Line	LNWR	26 July 1868
Over and Wharton-Winsford Junction	LNWR	1 June 1882
Crewe Independent Lines:		
Salop Goods Junction-Gresty Lane No 1	LNWR	c1899
Sorting Sidings Middle-Gresty Lane No 1	LNWR	c1899
Salop Goods Junction-Coal Yard	LNWR	14 September 1900
Salop Goods Junction-Basford Hall Junction	LNWR	14 September 1900
Salop Goods Junction-Sydney Bridge Junction	LNWR	24 March 1901
Sorting Sidings Middle-North Staffordshire Sidings	LNWR	c1903
Madeley Chord	BR	18 June 1962

Appendix 2

Closure Dates of Stations served by Crewe Stopping Trains and Pick-up Goods Trains

1. Stafford-Crewe

Great Bridgeford	8 August 1949 (Passenger)
Norton Bridge	Remains open
Badnall Wharf	22 June 1959 (Goods)
Standon Bridge	4 February 1952 (Passenger)
	4 January 1965 (Goods)
Whitmore	4 February 1952 (Passenger)
	8 June 1965 (Goods)
Madeley	4 February 1952 (Passenger)
	19 August 1963 (Goods)
Betley Road	1 October 1945 (Passenger)
	7 October 1963 (Goods)
Basford	1 July 1875 (Passenger)

2. Crewe-Warrington

Coppenhall	10 September 1840 (Passenger)
Minshull Vernon	2 March 1942 (Passenger)
Winsford	Remains open
Hartford	Remains open
Acton Bridge	Remains open
Preston Brook	1 April 1948 (Passenger); 1 September 1958 (Goods)
Moore	1 February 1943 (Passenger)

3. Crewe-Chester

Worleston	1 September 1952 (Passenger); 30 November 1959 (Goods)
Calveley	7 March 1960 (Passenger); 2 November 1964 (Goods)
Beeston Castle & Tarporley	4 January 1965 (Goods); 18 April 1966 (Passenger)
Tattenhall Road	15 June 1959 (Passenger); 1 March 1965 (Goods)
Waverton	15 June 1959 (Passenger); 1 March 1965 (Goods)

4. Crewe-Nantwich

Gresty Halt	c1923
Willaston	6 December 1954 (Passenger); 2 November 1964 (Goods)
Newcastle Crossing Halt	c1923

5. Crewe-Kidsgrove

Radway Green & Barthomley	6 July 1964 (Goods); 7 November 1966 (Passenger)

6. Goods Lines

Basford Hall Sorting Sidings-North Staffordshire Sidings	1 October 1984

25kv Electrification: Line Inaugural Dates

Crewe-Manchester Piccadilly via Stockport and Styal	12 October 1960
Crewe-Liverpool Lime Street	1 January 1962
Basford Hall marshalling yard	18 June 1962
Crewe-Stafford	7 January 1963
Euston-Crewe-Manchester/Liverpool services introduced	18 April 1966
Crewe-Stafford-Birmingham-Rugby services introduced	6 December 1966
Euston-West Midlands-North West services introduced	6 March 1967
Crewe-Weaver Junction-Preston services introduced	23 July 1973
Euston-Glasgow services introduced	6 May 1974

Appendix 3

Locomotive Allocations

The Crewe sheds in November 1945; peace had returned and steam was still unchallenged. There were nearly 250 steam locomotives allocated to North and South sheds, as well as only 13 diesels. It was a period when the enthusiastic spotter could have a field day: I remember a single day in June 1946 when I saw 160 locomotives that I had not seen before. This first allocation list is chosen in memory of them.

Crewe North Shed (5A)

Class 2P	4-4-0	322, 471, 492, 659, 660
Class 4P	4-4-0	1115, 1156, 1157, 1163, 1172
Class 4P	2-6-4T	2323, 2403, 2447, 2453, 2469, 2487, 2488, 2544, 2608
Class 5	4-6-0	4801, 4807, 4808, 4832, 4833, 4834, 4835, 4836, 4837, 4838, 4862, 4863, 4864, 4865, 4874, 4875, 4876, 4907, 4908, 4909, 5131, 5255, 5312, 5314, 5316, 5317, 5354, 5369, 5374, 5375, 5379, 5381, 5394, 5403, 5404, 5412, 5422, 5441, 5448, 5495
'Patriot'	4-6-0	5521 *Rhyl*, 5523 *Bangor*, 5530 *Sir Frank Ree*, 5532 *Illustrious*, 5539 *E. C. Trench*, 5540 *Sir Robert Turnbull* 5546 *Fleetwood*, 5548 *Lytham St Annes*, 5549, 5551
'Jubilee'	4-6-0	5555 *Quebec*, 5601 *British Guiana*, 5617 *Mauritius*, 5637 *Windward Islands*, 5666 *Cornwallis*, 5668 *Madden*, 5674 *Duncan*, 5675 *Hardy*, 5676 *Codrington*, 5681 *Aboukir*, 5683 *Hogue*, 5684 *Jutland*, 5686 *St Vincent*, 5687 *Neptune*, 5688 *Polyphemus*, 5689 *Ajax*, 5690 *Leander*, 5703 *Thunderer*, 5720 *Indomitable*, 5721 *Impregnable*, 5722 *Defence*, 5725 *Repulse*, 5733 *Novelty*

'Royal Scot'	4-6-0	6113 *Cameronian*, 6125 *3rd Carabinier*, 6126 *Royal Army Service Corps*, 6131 *The Royal Warwickshire Regiment*, 6132 *The King's Regiment Liverpool*, 6139 *The Welch Regiment*, 6146 *The Rifle Brigade*, 6147 *The Northamptonshire Regiment*, 6153 *The Royal Dragoon*, 6154 *The Hussar*, 6156 *The South Wales Borderer*, 6157 *The Royal Artilleryman*, 6160 *Queen Victoria's Rifleman*, 6161 *King's Own*, 6162 *Queen's Westminster Rifleman*, 6163 *Civil Service Rifleman*, 6165 *The Ranger (12th London Regiment)*, 6166 *London Rifle Brigade*, 6167 *The Hertfordshire Regiment*, 6168 *The Girl Guide*
'Princess Royal'	4-6-2	6201 *Princess Elizabeth*, 6204 *Princess Louise*, 6206 *Princess Marie Louise*, 6207 *Princess Arthur of Connaught*, 6208 *Princess Helena Victoria*, 6209 *Princess Beatrice*, 6210 *Lady Patricia*, 6211 *Queen Maud*, 6212 *Duchess of Kent*
'Princess Coronation'	4-6-2	6233 *Duchess of Sutherland*, 6234 *Duchess of Abercorn*, 6235 *City of Birmingham*, 6236 *City of Bradford*, 6252 *City of Leicester*
Class 2P	2-4-2T	6605, 6711, 6742

Total Allocation: 129 locomotives

Crewe South Shed (5B)

Class 2P	4-4-0	402, 405, 448
Class 5F	2-6-0	2785, 2885, 2920, 2946, 2947, 2949, 2950, 2952, 2955, 2956, 2960, 2961, 2962, 2968, 2974, 2980, 2982, 2983
Class 2F	0-6-0	3009, 3412, 3704
Class 4F	0-6-0	4064, 4126, 4300, 4453, 4595
Class 5	4-6-0	5020, 5028, 5033, 5034, 5037, 5038, 5044, 5048, 5059, 5060, 5064, 5067, 5069, 5072, 5073, 5074, 5089, 5097, 5108, 5134, 5143, 5146, 5148, 5181, 5183, 5195, 5197, 5198, 5235, 5236, 5239, 5240, 5248, 5254, 5264, 5270, 5271, 5300, 5305, 5384
Class 3F	0-6-0T	7266, 7280, 7309, 7330, 7344, 7362, 7384, 7414, 7416, 7444, 7445, 7451, 7523, 7524, 7526, 7602, 7608, 7616, 7633, 7653, 7665, 7680, 7681
Class 8F	2-8-0	8326, 8346, 8687, 8693
Class G2a 7F	0-8-0	8906, 9027, 9146, 9198, 9209, 9210, 9230, 9241, 9263, 9296, 9349, 9357
Class G2 7F	0-8-0	9396, 9445
Class 2F	0-6-0	22971, 22978
Class 2F	0-6-0	28458, 28583, 28614
Diesel-Electric	0-6-0	7074, 7076, 7079, 7087, 7088, 7090, 7092, 7095, 7120, 7121, 7122, 7123, 7124

Total Allocation: 115 steam locomotives
13 Diesel-Electrics

Crewe Gresty Lane — GWR sub-shed of Wellington
Final GWR allocation on 31 December 1947

Class 51xx	2-6-2T	4154, 5139
Class 57xx	0-6-0T	3749

Crewe — North Staffordshire Railway
Allocation in the 1900s was of three locomotives including:

Class 19	2-4-0	19

Locomotive Allocation as at September 1950

Crewe North Shed (5A)

Class 2P	4-4-0	40332, 40402, 40425, 40527, 40659, 40660
Class 4P	4-4-0	41112, 41115, 41160, 41167
Class 2P	2-6-2T	41229
Class 4P	2-6-4T	42308, 42677

'Black 5'	4-6-0	44678-44685, 44758, 44761-44766, 44770, 44771, 45217
'Patriot'	4-6-0	45502 *Royal Naval Division*, 45503 *The Leicestershire Regt*, 45504 *Royal Signals*, 45506 *The Royal Pioneer Corps*, 45507 *Royal Tank Corps*, 45510, 45511 *Isle of Man*, 45513, 45523 *Bangor*, 45528, 45529 *Stephenson*, 45535 *Sir Herbert Walker KCB*, 45543 *Home Guard*, 45546 *Fleetwood*, 45548 *Lytham St Annes*
'Jubilee'	4-6-0	45558 *Manitoba*, 45586 *Mysore*, 45592 *Indore*, 45606 *Falkland Islands*, 45634 *Trinidad*, 45647 *Sturdee*, 45666 *Cornwallis*, 45674 *Duncan*, 45678 *De Robeck*, 45684 *Jutland*, 45686 *St Vincent*, 45689 *Leander*, 45738 *Samson*
'Royal Scot'	4-6-0	46113 *Cameronian*, 46128 *The Lovat Scouts*, 46130 *The West Yorkshire Regiment*, 46146 *The Rifle Brigade*, 46155 *The Lancer*, 46157 *The Royal Artilleryman*
'Princess Royal'	4-6-2	46204 *Princess Louise*, 46206 *Princess Marie Louise*, 46207 *Princess Arthur of Connaught*, 46208 *Princess Helena Victoria*, 46209 *Princess Beatrice*, 46210 *Lady Patricia*, 46211 *Queen Maud*, 46212 *Duchess of Kent*
'Coronation'	4-6-2	46233 *Duchess of Sutherland*, 46234 *Duchess of Abercorn*, 46235 *City of Birmingham*, 46236 *City of Bradford*, 46243 *City of Glasgow*, 46246 *City of Manchester*, 46248 *City of Leeds*
Class 2MT	2-6-0	46457, 46458
Class 1P	2-4-2T	46680
Class 2F	0-6-0	58388, 58429

Total Allocation: 85 steam locomotives

Crewe South (5B)		
Class 5F	2-6-0	42773, 42785, 42810, 42811, 42815, 42856, 42920, 42926, 42939, 42950, 42952, 42955, 42956, 42968, 42972, 42980, 42983, 42984
Class 3F	0-6-0	43189, 43207
Class 4F	0-6-0	44126, 44300, 44301, 44452
'Black 5'	4-6-0	45006, 45013, 45030, 45038, 45044, 45048, 45060, 45067, 45073, 45093, 45108, 45131, 45134, 45148, 45185, 45189, 45195, 45198, 45239, 45240, 45254, 45270, 45271, 45294, 45300, 45301, 45369
Class 3F	0-6-0T	47266, 47280, 47330, 47344, 47384, 47414, 47431, 47450, 47523, 47524, 47526, 47590, 57595, 47633, 47661, 47662, 47670, 47680
Class 8F	2-8-0	48248-48257, 48259-48263, 48286-48292, 48294-48297, 48757
Class G2a	0-8-0	49210, 49230, 49319
Class G2	0-8-0	49407
Class 0F	0-4-0T	51204, 51221
Diesel-Electric	0-6-0	12000-12002, 12018, 12033-12037, 12049-12055

Total Allocation: 102 steam locomotives
16 Diesel-Electrics

Locomotive Allocation as at November 1960

Crewe North (5A)		
Class 2MT	2-6-2T	41212, 41220, 41229
Class 4MT	2-6-4T	42079, 42575
Class 5MT	2-6-0	42776, 42815, 42940, 42958, 42963, 42966, 42968
'Black 5'	4-6-0	44678-44681, 44683-44685, 44714, 44759, 44761-44765, 44770, 44844, 44911, 45003, 45004, 45021, 45033, 45037, 45073, 45132, 45189, 45235, 45240, 45243, 45250, 45254, 45257, 45289, 45311, 45348, 45369, 45379, 45446
'Patriot'	4-6-0	45528, 45529 *Stephenson*, 45534 *E. Tootal Broadhurst*, 45545 *Planet*
'Jubilee'	4-6-0	45553 *Canada*, 45556 *Nova Scotia*, 45591 *Udaipur*, 45595 *Southern Rhodesia*, 45604 *Ceylon*, 45628 *Somaliland*, 45629 *Straits*

126

		Settlements, 45630 *Swaziland*, 45634 *Trinidad*, 45643 *Rodney*, 45655 *Keith*, 45666 *Cornwallis*, 45670 *Howard of Effingham*, 45674 *Duncan*, 45676 *Codrington*, 45684 *Jutland*, 45689 *Ajax*, 45726 *Vindictive*, 45736 *Phoenix*, 45737 *Atlas*
'Royal Scot'	4-6-0	46110 *Grenadier Guardsman*, 46111 *Royal Fusilier*, 46115 *Scots Guardsman*, 46116 *Irish Guardsman*, 46125 *3rd Carabinier*, 46127 *Old Contemptibles*, 46128 *The Lovat Scouts*, 46129 *The Scottish Horse*, 46134 *The Cheshire Regiment*, 46135 *The East Lancashire Regiment*, 46136 *The Border Regiment*, 46149 *The Middlesex Regiment*, 46152 *The King's Dragoon Guardsman*, 46155 *The Lancer*, 46159 *The Royal Air Force*, 46164 *The Artists' Rifleman*, 46166 *London Rifle Brigade*, 46169 *The Boy Scout*,
'Princess Royal'	4-6-2	46200 *The Princess Royal*, 46205 *Princess Victoria*, 46209 *Princess Beatrice*, 46212 *Duchess of Kent*
'Coronation'	4-6-2	46220 *Coronation*, 46221 *Queen Elizabeth*, 46228 *Duchess of Rutland*, 46229 *Duchess of Hamilton*, 46235 *City of Birmingham*, 46241 *City of Edinburgh*, 46248 *City of Leeds*, 46249 *City of Sheffield*, 46251 *City of Nottingham*, 46254 *City of Stoke-on-Trent*, 46256 *Sir William A. Stanier FRS*
Class 8P	4-6-2	71000 *Duke of Gloucester*
Class 2MT	2-6-0	78030
'Peak'	1Co-Co1	D3 *Skiddaw*, D8 *Penyghent*, D9 *Snowdon*, D68, D69
Type 4	1Co-Co1	D220, D224, D227, D230, D297-D301, D305-D307

Total Allocation: 108 steam locomotives
17 Diesel-Electrics

Crewe South (5B)

Class 5MT	2-6-0	42944, 42948, 42959, 42952, 42955, 42956, 42959, 42961, 42962, 42964, 42972, 42975, 42979, 42980, 42983, 42984
Class 3F	0-6-0	43464
Class 4F	0-6-0	44301, 44592
'Black 5'	4-6-0	44713, 44832, 44834, 44868, 45000-45002, 45045, 45048, 45067, 45074, 45128, 45130, 45142, 45148, 45149, 45198, 45248, 45270, 45291, 45298-45300, 45391, 45403, 45494
Class 3F	0-6-0T	47280, 47310, 47338, 47348, 47354, 47384, 47391, 47395, 47397, 47400, 47414, 47431, 47445, 47450, 47467, 47482, 47516, 47523, 47524, 47525, 47529, 47601, 47608, 47661, 47664, 47677, 47680
Class 8F	2-8-0	48085, 48252, 48255, 48257, 48262, 48292, 48294, 48297, 48423, 48502, 48516, 48548, 48626, 48630, 48633, 48655, 48659, 48692, 48693, 48729, 48734, 48743
Class G2a	0-8-0	49158
Class G2	0-8-0	49407
Drewry	0-6-0	D 2221, D2236
Diesel-Electric	0-6-0	D3089, D3175, D3245, D3291, D3292, D3367, D3583, D3584, D3763, 12000, 12001, 12005, 12009-12011, 12020, 12021, 12025, 12031, 12032

Total Allocation: 96 steam locomotives
22 diesel locomotives

Locomotive Allocation as at November 1976

Crewe Diesel Depot (CD)

Class 08	0-6-0	036/055/068/080/088, 112/123/125/132, 220/222/289, 329/382/390/395, 416/468/469/470/475, 631/633/635/694, 701/737/739, 802/843
Class 24	Bo-Bo	023/035/036/047/052/057/063/081/082/087/091, 133/134
Class 25	Bo-Bo	041-043/055/056/061/081, 111/148/150-153/156-169/184/185, 264/290-294/299, 304/306/307/322/323/326/327

Class 47	Co-Co	034/040/048-051/074/094/095, 182/190-199, 204/205/214/227/228/249/262/264/266/267/280/290, 337-340/342/344-346/348-353/358/359/367/369/436-456/480/481/490-492, 501/503/515/529/539/555

Total Allocation: 168 locomotives

Crewe Electric Depot (CE)

Class 84	Bo-Bo	001-010
Class 85	Bo-Bo	001-040
Class 304	EMU	016-025/027-035

Total Allocation: 50 locomotives
19 Electric Multiple-Units

Bibliography

Baker, A. & Morrison, G., *Crewe Sheds*
Barrie, D.S., *The Euston & Crewe Companion*
Biddle, G., *The Railway Surveyors*
Biddle, G., *Victorian Stations*
Bolger, P., *BR Steam Motive Power Depots LMR*
Bradshaw's, *Railway Manual & Shareholders' Guide* (Various years)
British Rail (LMR), *Change at Crewe* (1960)
British Rail (LMR), *All Change at Crewe* (1985)
Chaloner, W. H., *The Social & Economic Development of Crewe 1780-1923*
Christiansen, R, *Forgotten Railways: Volume 11 Severn Valley & Welsh Border*
Christiansen, R., & Miller, R. W., *The North Staffordshire Railway*
Christiansen, R. & Miller, R. W., *The Cambrian Railways Volumes 1 and 2*
Clinker, C. R., *Clinker's Register of Closed Passenger Stations & Goods Depots in England, Scotland & Wales*
Crewe Guardian, The Jubilee of Crewe 1887
Crewe & Nantwich Borough Council, *Official Guide*
Foster, R. D., *A Pictorial Record of L.N.W.R. Signalling*
Gillham, J. C., *The Age of the Electric Train*
Hawkins, C & Reeve, G., *LMS Engine Sheds Volume 1*
Jacobs, G. & Yonge, J., *British Rail Track Diagrams 4 London Midland Region*
Lewthwaite, G. C., *Branch Line Index* (1991)
'Manifold', *The North Staffordshire Railway*
Measom, G., *The Official Illustrated Guide to the North-Western Railway* (1861)
Morriss, R. K., *Rail Centres: Shrewsbury*
Neele, G. P., *Railway Reminiscences*
Nock, O. S., *The London & North Western Railway*
Nock, O. S., *LMS Steam*
Nock, O. S., *North Western*
Nock, O. S., *60 Years of West Coast Express Running*
Reed, B., *Crewe to Carlisle*
Reed, B., *Crewe Locomotive Works and its Men*
Shaw, G., *The Official Tourists' Picturesque Guide to the London & North Western Railway* (1876)
Signalling Record Society, *British Railway Layout Plans of the 1950s from the John Swift collection. Volume 4: ex-North Staffordshire Railway Lines*
Talbot, E., *A Pictorial Tribute to Crewe: Crewe Works in the Age of Steam*
Talbot, E., *LNWR Miscellany Volumes 1 & 2*
Webster, N. W., *Britain's First Trunk Line: The Grand Junction Railway*

Also consulted: Journals and magazines of the Branch Line Society, Manchester Locomotive Society, Railway & Canal Historical Society, Railway Correspondence & Travel Society, Stephenson Locomotive and Wirral Railway Circle.
Notes for several railtours of the Branch Line and Stephenson Locomotive Societies proved valuable sources.
Articles on Crewe are to be found in many magazines on railways. Some of the most detailed are in early issues of *The Railway Magazine*.
Timetables are another source of useful material and I consulted a number of issues of *Bradshaw's*, and those of British Rail, the Cambrian Railways, GWR, LMS, LNWR and NSR and also Working Timetables and Sectional Appendices of BR and several companies.